J THE
OURNEY
BECKONS

Reflections on the Way of the Cross

THE
JOURNEY
BECKONS

Edited by
Mary Ellen Ashcroft and Holly Bridges

Augsburg

MINNEAPOLIS

THE JOURNEY BECKONS
Reflections on the Way of the Cross

First Augsburg Books edition. Originally published as *Bearing Our Sorrows*, copyright © 1994 Mary Ellen Ashcroft and Holly Bridges.

Cover design by Nicole Sletten
Cover image from the Dutch Masters/Planet Art. Used by permission.

Library of Congress Cataloging-in-Publication Data
   [Bearing our sorrows]
The journey beckons: reflections on the way of the cross / [edited by] Mary Ellen Ashcroft and Holly Bridges.—1st Augsburg Books ed.
   p. cm.
   Originally published: Bearing our sorrows. 1st ed. San Francisco: HarperSanFrancisco, c1993.
   Includes bibliographical references and index.
   ISBN 0-8066-4033-2 (alk. paper)
   1. Consolation. 2. Crosses. 3. Stations of the Cross. I. Ashcroft, Mary Ellen, 1952– II. Bridges, Holly, 1954– III. Title.

BV4905.2.B335 2000
242'.4—dc21
                                       99-052799

Manufactured in the U.S.A.   AF 9-4033

04   03   02   01   00   1   2   3   4   5   6   7   8   9   10

*To those whose lives and choices have been shaped
by creative and courageous understandings of the cross*

Contents

Almighty God, whose most dear Son went not up to joy but first he suffered pain, and entered not into glory before he was crucified: mercifully grant that we, walking in the way of the cross, may find it none other than the way of life and peace; through Jesus Christ your Son our Lord, who lives and reigns with you and the Holy Spirit, one God, for ever and ever. Amen.

BOOK OF COMMON PRAYER,
COLLECT FOR MONDAY IN HOLY WEEK

Preface

$\mathcal{W}$e all move from birth to death and, as we travel, we encounter separation, loss, uncertainty, growth, danger, death. To be human is to confront these realities. They are the places of risk, where we pause or teeter, where we either retreat to the safety of old habits and securities or take the bold leap to trust. Whether our pain and difficulties are freely chosen or thrust upon us, we have some choice about how to respond. We have freedom to shape meaning, to find purpose as we bear our struggles. And as Christians, we have a model.

At the heart of the Christian faith is the choice Jesus made to journey bearing the cross. "Surely he has borne our griefs and carried our sorrows" (Isaiah 53:4). These words from the prophet Isaiah have been used since Christianity's earliest days to describe the way Jesus lived and the way he died. During his life, contrary to the pull of natural inclinations, Jesus chose pain over ease; nonconformity over conformity; surprise over predictability; insecurity over security. In choosing to bear his cross, Jesus affirmed that way as life-giving, as redemptive. His way was not passive resignation to circumstances or fate. Jesus bore his cross, his life, not like a packhorse bears a cumbersome load. He bore it like a woman bears a child, bringing it to birth with strength and love.

But when we, his followers, join the journey toward the cross, as Christ did, what does that entail? *The Journey Beckons* offers a view of the panoramic responses of Christians to this question. We are reminded that we do not struggle alone. Not only do we follow Christ; we walk with fellow Christians. From all over the world and across the span of twenty centuries, the voices collected here invite us to stop and meditate on the way of the cross and its implications for our lives.

We have gathered these responses as if we, like generations before us, were on pilgrimage. It is an ancient, symbolic way for Christians to express their desire to follow Jesus, to experience his passion, to bear his cross with him. Pilgrims traveled together—pressing forward as a group, expecting to find healing along the way, to gain insight from their stops at holy places, perhaps to watch a mystery play and re-present Christ's passion. They read the windows of the great cathedrals to learn the stories that undergirded their faith.

For those pilgrims who could not undertake a lengthy trip, the service of the Stations of the Cross, held inside or near a church, became a pilgrimage made accessible. The journey was placed in a ritual setting.

The Journey Beckons likewise takes us on a pilgrimage. In the company of Christians who have taken up the cross, we stop to learn from them at each station. Readers of the collection needn't be familiar with the traditional Stations of the Cross, however. The stations are used here as signposts on the way, pointing to larger themes; they are stopping places, where we might ponder the connections between our experience and that of others.

The collection progresses from the realization that sacrifice may be necessary and from definitions of the cross and continues with the consequences of taking it up. During the journey, the stopping places invite readers to experience communal solidarity, to consider the implications of a suffering God, to fathom our experiences of vulnerability. By the end we come to see that life can come from death, that Jesus remains present in our situations, and that there are joys to celebrate.

The Journey Beckons touches on issues that are timeless for Christians, such as choosing to abandon ourselves to God radically, deciding to forgo apparent security and control, dying to old relationships and to old selves, finding courage in adversity, making sense out of suffering, defying the powers that intend our destruction, trying to understand the nature of our God in the storms of unpredictable tragedy—the loss of a child, devastating divorce, grave illness—choosing to trust that life is stronger than death. This collection is also useful to readers who want to reflect on Christ's passion and resurrection.

How to Use This Collection

These readings are companions on a journey, like a traveler's guide. They are not meant to be speed-read and put aside. As the traveler arrives at a station, she may have an immediate response to the sight of a cathedral, and then need time to stand back for a wider view or to sit contemplating one stained-glass window. Here are several suggestions of ways you can stop for a longer, more considered look, whether you are using the book for individual devotional study or for group discussion.

For Individual Use

You may want to read several quotations each morning and return to them for reflection during the day. Or you may want to read several in the evening and turn them into prayer as you fall asleep.

Use a journal to record your feelings, responses, and insights. To start keeping a journal with this book (or to continue a long-standing habit), respond to the readings by writing answers to questions like these:

• What stands out for me from this particular quotation?

• Why does this idea stand out to me? Does it speak to some circumstance in my life? Does this writer have a new way of looking at an issue?

• How does this new perspective or insight make me feel? How does it touch some personal situation or relationship?

• What does this truth remind me of—perhaps something I've learned before or something someone said to me or a passage from Scripture?

You may want to turn your reflections into a written prayer: "God, I ask that I may more deeply understand what it is to . . ." or "Help me to live this out in my relationship to . . ."

If the reading is already a prayer, you might expand it. After one line, insert your own concerns. For instance, begin with the line, "God, our sustainer, you have called your people out into the wilderness . . ." and add, "God, my wilderness right now is my future. I want to find ways of seeing you with me there . . ."

For Group Use

If you are using the book in a study or prayer or support group, you may wish to schedule one chapter at a time for discussion. All members bring a question that was raised by one or more of the readings, which the group discusses. Then each member may want to explain which reading she found most helpful and why, and tell how she hopes to make this insight meaningful in her situation. The group could then turn these reflections into prayer.

We invite you to join the company of pilgrims who have embraced the way of the cross. Traveling with grace, creativity, and integrity, they illumine the path for us.

NOTE: Although we believe that many of the writers in this book would use inclusive language if they were writing today, we have preserved their words as they were written. Also, dates are omitted following the names of authors who are alive today.

CHAPTER 1

The Journey Beckons
(Jesus Is Condemned)

*J*esus stood silent when he was condemned by Pilate, his death on the cross now inevitable. In one sense the condemnation was the beginning of the end, the first stop on the way to Golgotha. But in another sense Pilate's verdict confirmed Jesus' calling, adding legal weight to a decision Jesus had made long before—perhaps when he saw the injustice and hypocrisy of the temple hucksters and took a stand against them, or perhaps when he struggled in Gethsemane with his desire to avoid the cross.

But Pilate's condemnation brought a flash of clarity—Jesus saw his way ahead. We too experience the flash of realization, the moment when we see the path and know we will not turn back, that there are no guarantees.

Our realization may provoke us to turn from living "as if Christ did not rise from the dead," as Alexander Schmemann says in this chapter. Or

1

our epiphany may reveal that we must die—perhaps not yet physically—but to a relationship or idea to which we've clung or a false self we've cherished. Our realization may be the moment in which we begin to be willing, as Raissa Maritain says, to "live in the whirlwind, without keeping back anything for ourselves," or where we accept the calling to be sent into "the pain of a world where people die," as Frederick Buechner describes it.

Most of us find ourselves longing to echo Peter's words, "Not you, Lord, and certainly not the cross!" The voices in this chapter invite us to embrace the way of the cross. Janet Morley reminds us that God has called us "into the wilderness to travel . . . unknown ways." Gertrud Mueller Nelson invites us to find the place in God where we "remain very still at the center of life's paradoxes, nailed in place between the opposites out of which we once built our lives."

Let us begin the journey here, asking God to use the voices of this community to illuminate our way of the cross. We know that with an insight comes a choice. Let us listen as they encourage us to abandon our securities, "to undertake the journey without understanding the destination," as Michael Leunig says, to face our hard callings, to prepare to be broken.

*T*he cross is not the terrible end to an otherwise god-fearing and happy life, but it meets us at the beginning of our communion with Christ. When Christ calls a man, he bids him come and die. It may be a death like that of the first disciples who had to leave home and work to follow him, or it may be a death like Luther's, who had to leave the monastery and go out into the world. But it is the same death every time—death in Jesus Christ, the death of the old man at his call. Jesus' summons to the rich young man was calling him to die, because only the man who is dead to his own will can follow Christ. In fact every command of Jesus is a call to die, with all our affections and lusts. But we do not want to die, and therefore Jesus Christ and his call are necessarily our death as well as our life. The call to discipleship, the baptism in the name of Jesus Christ means both death and life.

DIETRICH BONHOEFFER
GERMANY (1906–1945)

*W*hat needs to die is not the real self, but the false one, the self that thinks it is whole and complete when, in fact, it is all in pieces. Identity and calling are the first great uncertainties we question as we come to the deserts of our life. As we approach the age of forty—that mystical Lenten number—we learn the pain of the mid-life transition. Not so very long ago, people had the grace to die around age forty. That was about as long as one could physically hold out, having spent up all energy at survival. Today we live well past age forty. We live at least twice as long, and at mid-life we are asked to die on a different level. Identity, vocation, motives, judgments, relationships all come into question again. We reach a vantage point, like standing on a mountain top, where we are given the opportunity to look at our past and look into our future all at once. We look back and see the roads not taken, the strokes of luck, the missteps, the relationships failed or avoided or taken for granted.

... We head into the downhill side of our life and are aware of our death. On the road, we die a hundred little deaths. We die when we reach out to others, and there is no hope of recognition or repayment. We give up our control of others and we give them the life they are meant to live. Our children are not our creations. We forgive and ask forgiveness. We realize and accept that our marriage may never be the fantasy dream we planned out for ourselves. ...

We know what it is to be torn in two directions, no, in four directions. We know now why the cross is the Christian symbol of suffering necessary to wholeness. So this is why it has been held up before us all these years, so that we recognize it when its mystery becomes a reality in our own lives. Now we have to remain very still at the center of life's paradoxes, nailed in place between the opposites out of which we once built our lives.

GERTRUD MUELLER NELSON
UNITED STATES

*I*s it not our daily experience . . . that all the time we lose and betray the "new life" which we received as a gift, and that in fact we live as if Christ did not rise from the dead, as if that unique event had no meaning whatsoever for us? All this because of our weakness, because of the impossibility for us to live constantly by "faith, hope, and love" on that level to which Christ raised us when he said: "Seek ye, first of all, the Kingdom of God and His righteousness." We simply forget all this—so busy are we, so immersed in our daily preoccupations—and because we forget, we fail. And through this forgetfulness, failure, and sin, our life becomes "old" again—petty, dark, and ultimately meaningless—a meaningless journey toward a meaningless end. We manage to forget even death and then, all of a sudden, in the midst of our "enjoying life" it comes to us: horrible, inescapable, senseless. We may from time to time acknowledge and confess our various "sins," yet we cease to refer our life to that new life which Christ revealed and gave to us. Indeed, we live as if He never came. This is the only real sin, the sin of all sins, the bottomless sadness and tragedy of our nominal Christianity.

If we realize this, then we may understand what Easter is and why it needs and presupposes Lent. For we may then understand that the liturgical traditions of the Church, all its cycles and services, exist, first of all, in order to help us recover the vision and the taste of that *new life* which we so easily lose and betray, so that we may repent and return to it.

ALEXANDER SCHMEMANN
UNITED STATES

*G*od help us to change. To change ourselves and to change our world. To know the need for it. To deal with the pain of it. To feel the joy of it. To undertake the journey without understanding the destination. The art of gentle revolution. Amen

MICHAEL LEUNIG

AUSTRALIA

*W*e all have to be born again, not once but many times if we are to enter the kingdom. This deep longing for growth was and is the central force of the Christian pilgrimage. The Christian is always being born anew. The pressure to grow is inherent and yet we fight it. . . . There is a self within each one of us aching to be born, a self burdened with contradiction, and everything (I mean *everything*) we do is designed to alleviate the discomfort caused by contrary forces within us, . . . We, like the heroes of old, have to enter a mythological cycle of descent and return, of death and resurrection. Unless some of us are willing to make the journey, I see little hope for the church, for the world, for all those things that make genuine humanity at least a possibility. Without such pioneers, however reluctant they may be, there is no glimpse of real joy.

ALAN JONES
UNITED STATES

*I*n the year that King Uzziah died, or in the year that John F. Kennedy died, or in the year that somebody you loved died, you go into the temple if that is your taste, or you hide your face in the little padded temple of your hands, and a voice says, "Whom shall I send into the pain of a world where people die?" and if you are not careful, you may find yourself answering, "Send me." You may hear the voice say, "Go." Just *go*.

FREDERICK BUECHNER

UNITED STATES

*T*he call to grace in its ultimate form is a summons to be one with God, to assume peership with God. Hence it is a call to total adulthood. We are accustomed to imagining the experience of conversion or sudden call to grace as an "Oh, joy!" phenomenon. In my experience, more often than not it is, at least partially, an "Oh, shit" phenomenon. At the moment we finally listen to the call we may say, "Oh, thank you, Lord"; or we may say, "O Lord, I am not worthy"; or we may say, "O Lord, do I have to?"

M. SCOTT PECK
UNITED STATES

*W*e walk in darkness, risking bruising ourselves against a thousand obstacles. But we know that "God is Love" and trust in God as our light. I have the feeling that what is asked of us is to live in the whirlwind, without keeping back anything for ourselves, neither rest nor friendships nor health nor leisure—to pray incessantly and that even without leisure—in fact to let ourselves pitch and toss in the waves of divine will till the day when it will say: "That's enough."

RAISSA MARITAIN
FRANCE (1883–1960)

*G*od, our sustainer,
You have called out your people into
the wilderness
to travel your unknown ways.
Make us strong to leave behind false
security and comfort,
and give us new hope in our calling;
that the desert may blossom as a
rose,
and your promises may be fulfilled in us.
In the name of Jesus Christ, Amen

JANET MORLEY
ENGLAND

CHAPTER 2

Embracing the Cross
(Jesus Takes Up the Cross)

*T*he act of Jesus taking up the cross has for centuries been held out to believers as an example to be imitated. When we answer the call to embrace the cross, what are we implying?

As Christianity's central symbol, the cross must declare its stark reality as a means of execution. Elaborate fretwork or a painter's technique may sometimes cushion the offense of this reality, but the cross cannot escape its connections with suffering and death. Christianity is the religion of the cross; it is an emphatic rejection, however, of masochistic suffering and self-torment, say the authors in this chapter as they seek to define the cross.

The cross is a "choice made by free persons" and a rejection "of death in all its forms," says Gustavo Gutiérrez. It is the price of courage. The example of Jesus' embrace of the cross gives us "the wisdom to differentiate between the suffering imposed by an oppressor and the suffering that is the consequence of one's stand for justice and human dignity," according to Chung Hyun Kyung.

The cross is much more than some annoyance: the in-law who came to visit for a week but ended up staying indefinitely; the crotchety committee member who always derails meetings; the dull, routine task. This is to confuse the merely irksome with the truly profound nature of God's call to faithfulness.

Jesus' decision not to flee from the cross entailed a clear-sighted commitment to a goal that would necessarily involve suffering and self-denial. As we follow Jesus, we too may find ourselves presented with opportunities for rejecting cowardice, as Frederick Douglass did, or, as with Maggie Ross, for wrestling "against our desire to pander to our own egos" and choosing to let go. We may find ourselves forced to distinguish between the sham suffering of our self-absorption and the real suffering that results from our sincere concern for another.

When believers freely choose to take up the cross, we are not endorsing suffering. Nor are we trifling. We are responding with radical openness to God's call—a call to new life, a call to participate in a new order.

*T*he cross is the most peculiar and distinctive feature of Christian faith, but Christian spirituality is not formally a spirituality of suffering; rather, it is a spirituality focused on the following of Jesus. Not all suffering is specifically Christian; only that which flows from the following of Jesus is.

JON SOBRINO
EL SALVADOR

*T*he agony in the Garden of Gethsemani [is] the agony our lives reflect as we attempt to listen to the voice that speaks against the desire to pander to our egos, our selfish appetites, our laziness and apathy, and the potential for wickedness that lurks in our depths.

MAGGIE ROSS
UNITED STATES

*I*f we have to suffer to qualify as children of God, some of us will need to revise our vision of the good life. Most of us will look at suffering and wonder, *why?* Jesus tells us to look at suffering and wonder, *why not?* . . .

It is not as if any old suffering qualifies us as the children of God. It is not as if it will be all right merely because we have been walloped with the bare fist of fate. The catch is we have to suffer *with* someone else who suffers. Why not put it concretely and Christianly? We need to suffer *with Jesus.* We are "fellow heirs [of God] with Christ, provided we suffer with him." This is the catch. Some catch!

LEWIS B. SMEDES
UNITED STATES

*T*he Way of the Cross is a choice made by free persons who reject death in all its forms: physical death, the death of egotistical sinfulness, and the death involved in disregarding and forgetting others.

GUSTAVO GUTIÉRREZ
PERU

I humbly bless his gracious Providence, who gave me his treasure in an earthen vessel, and trained me up in the school of affliction, and taught me the cross of Christ so soon; that I might be rather . . . a cross-bearer, than a cross-maker or imposer.

RICHARD BAXTER
ENGLAND (1615–1691)

The Cross of Christ should become the very substance of our life. No doubt this is what Christ meant when he advised his friends to bear their cross each day, and not, as people seem to think nowadays, simply that one should be resigned about one's little daily troubles—which, by an almost sacrilegious abuse of language, people sometimes refer to as crosses.

SIMONE WEIL
FRANCE (1909–1943)

*G*od does not need our sacrifices. He does not like his children to torment themselves, hurt themselves, become gloomy. He loves only to give, and if he calls us to loving and voluntary sacrifice, it is because he is so much a Father that he wants us to share everything: he wants to invite us to know his joy, to imitate his generosity. He wants to give us the capacity of giving.

LOUIS EVELY

BELGIUM

*J*esus is neither a masochist who enjoys suffering, nor a father's boy who blindly does what he is told to do. On the contrary, Jesus is a compassionate man of integrity who identified himself with the oppressed. He "stood for all he taught and did" and took responsibility for the consequences of his choice even at the price of his life. This image of Jesus' suffering gives Asian women the wisdom to differentiate between the suffering imposed by an oppressor and the suffering that is the consequence of one's stand for justice and human dignity.

CHUNG HYUN KYUNG

SOUTH KOREA

*M*r. Covey entered the stable with a long rope; and just as I was half out of the loft, he caught hold of my legs, and was about tying me. As soon as I found what he was up to, I gave a sudden spring, and as I did so, he holding to my legs, I was brought sprawling on the stable floor. Mr. Covey seemed now to think he had me, and could do what he pleased; but at this moment—from whence came the spirit I don't know—I resolved to fight. . . . We were at it for nearly two hours. Covey at length let me go, puffing and blowing at a great rate, saying that if I had not resisted, he would not have whipped me half so much. The truth was, that he had not whipped me at all. I considered him as getting entirely the worst end of the bargain; for he had drawn no blood from me, but I had from him. The whole six months afterwards, that I spent with Mr. Covey, he never laid the weight of his finger upon me in anger. . . .

This battle with Mr. Covey was the turning-point in my career as a slave. It rekindled the few expiring embers of freedom, and revived within me a sense of my own manhood. It recalled the departed self-confidence, and inspired me again with a determination to be free. The gratification afforded by the triumph was a full compensation for whatever else might follow, even death itself. He only can understand the deep satisfaction which I experienced, who has himself repelled by force the bloody arm of slavery. I felt as I never felt before. It was a glorious resurrection, from the tomb of slavery, to the heaven of freedom. My long-crushed spirit rose, cowardice departed, bold defiance took its place; and I now resolved that, however long I might remain a slave in form, the day had passed forever when I could be a slave in fact.

FREDERICK DOUGLASS
UNITED STATES (1817–1895)

*I*n later years [the ceremony of]
piercing in the back near the shoulders
was like carrying the cross.
That is why they did it, then.
Unknown to them
they were practicing that
until Christianity came
and they realized
it meant carrying the cross.
They had no answer for the connection,
only that the true vision
of the medicine man
inspired them to do this.

ᎬDGAR ᎡED CLOUD
ᑌNITED STATES

CHAPTER 3

Counting the Cost
(Jesus Falls the First Time)

We often think of Christianity as a blessed way of life—and so it is. But in our focus on Christian blessings, many of us may become like the fun-loving tourists about whom Annie Dillard writes, who sail along oblivious to the gravity and even danger of the journey. The voyage on which we have embarked includes not only meals in the captain's dining room and misty views over a polished deck rail, not only the postcards and souvenirs. Our journey will have parts that are hard to stomach, experiences that will make us different people—the rolling deck and the shantytown.

Jesus himself may have set out on the way of the cross without fully realizing that the path before him stretched long: that it twisted with bewildering bends and hid many holes for stumbling. When we fall, as Jesus fell the first time and struggled to his feet, we may begin to realize the painfulness of our choice. The writers in this chapter have made a similar discovery—that the way of the cross is costly. This is a pilgrimage, not a tour.

When we signed up for this journey and embraced the way of the cross, we perhaps didn't fully realize the implications. Our pilgrimage will change us along the way. We will arrive as different people from the ones who left: we will be more like Christ. That's the point of the trip.

Jesus saw the cost. He urged himself to his feet to move on. The writers in this chapter invite us, with God's help, to do the same. They help us as we count the cost, to reaffirm our choice to be pilgrims. They remind us that whoever would cling to life will find that life slips by.

But as pilgrims we need to be reminded that the way is demanding, and that we must refuse to retreat into comforts and securities but instead resolve to "dance within the storm," as Kathy Galloway elegantly puts it in this chapter.

As we move in the direction demanded of us—whether it is the call to be creative or the daring, as W. E. B. DuBois says, to "do the deed"—we realize that spiritual growth carries with it a high price.

O God, your Son chose the path which led to pain before joy and the cross before glory. Plant his cross in our hearts, so that in its power and love we may come at last to joy and glory; through your Son, Jesus Christ our Lord.

LUTHERAN BOOK OF WORSHIP

*I*f your goal is to avoid pain and escape suffering, I would not advise you to seek higher levels of consciousness or spiritual evolution. First, you cannot achieve them without suffering, and second, insofar as you do achieve them, you are likely to be called on to serve in ways more painful to you, or at least demanding of you, than you can now imagine. Then why desire to evolve at all, you may ask. If you ask this question, perhaps you do not know enough of joy.

M. SCOTT PECK
UNITED STATES

*T*oo many people, when they hear the word *creativity,* imagine that a life of creativity is a life of tiptoeing through the tulips, a life of "doing nothing" or of pure enjoyment. In fact, such people only reveal their ignorance of birthing. For all birthing involves labor pains. All creativity involves destruction and deep suffering. It was precisely Jesus' creative reworking of Israelite religion that led to his crucifixion and death. . . . Because the artist does not dwell on the pain—as an ascetic so often does—but on the ecstasy of birthing, as Jesus did, the price the artist pays for creativity often goes uncounted or becomes distorted—as is the case in too much of the fall/redemption remembering of the cross of Jesus Christ. A significant contribution to salvation that is made by Jesus' crucifixion is his invitation to be courageous enough to create. And to pay the price.

MATTHEW FOX
UNITED STATES

*F*orgive us, O Lord, we acknowledge ourselves as type of the
    common man,
Of the men and women who shut the door and sit by the
    fire;
Who fear the blessing of God, the loneliness of the night of
    God, the surrender required, the deprivation inflicted;
Who fear the injustice of men less than the justice of God;
Who fear the hand at the window, the fire in the thatch, the
    fist in the tavern, the push into the canal,
Less than we fear the love of God.
We acknowledge our trespass, our weakness, our fault; we
    acknowledge
That the sin of the world is upon our heads; that the blood
    of the martyrs and the agony of the saints
Is upon our heads.

T. S. ELIOT
ENGLAND (1888–1965)

*W*hy do we people in churches seem like cheerful, brainless tourists on a packaged tour of the Absolute?

The tourists are having coffee and doughnuts on Deck C. Presumably someone is minding the ship, correcting the course, avoiding icebergs and shoals, fueling the engines, watching the radar screen, noting weather reports radioed in from shore. No one would dream of asking the tourists to do these things. Alas, among the tourists on Deck C, drinking coffee and eating doughnuts, we find the captain, and all the ship's officers, and all the ship's crew. The officers chat; they swear; they wink a bit at slightly raw jokes, just like regular people. The crew members have funny accents. The wind seems to be picking up.

On the whole, I do not find Christians, outside of the catacombs, sufficiently sensible of conditions. Does anyone have the foggiest idea what sort of power we so blithely invoke? Or, as I suspect, does no one believe a word of it? The churches are children playing on the floor with their chemistry sets, mixing up a batch of TNT to kill a Sunday morning. It is madness to wear ladies' straw hats and velvet hats to church; we should all be wearing crash helmets. Ushers should issue life preservers and signal flares; they should lash us to our pews. For the sleeping god may wake someday and take offense, or the waking god may draw us out to where we can never return.

ANNIE DILLARD

UNITED STATES

Do not retreat into your private world,
That place of safety, sheltered from the storm,
Where you may tend your garden, seek your soul,
And rest with loved ones where the fire burns warm.

To tend a garden is a precious thing,
But dearer still the one where all may roam,
The weeds of poison, poverty and war,
Demand your care, who call the earth your home.

To seek your soul it is a precious thing,
But you will never find it on your own,

Only among the clamour, threat and pain
Of other people's need will love be known.

To rest with loved ones is a precious thing,
But peace of mind exacts a higher cost,
Your children will not rest and play in quiet,
While they still hear the crying of the lost.

Do not retreat into your private world,
There are more ways than firesides to keep warm;
There is no shelter from the rage of life,
So meet its eye, and dance within the storm.

KATHY GALLOWAY
IONA COMMUNITY, SCOTLAND

*S*uch grace is *costly* because it calls us to follow, and it is *grace* because it calls us to follow *Jesus Christ.* It is costly because it costs a man his life, and it is grace because it gives a man the only true life. It is costly because it condemns sin, and grace because it justifies the sinner. Above all, it is *costly* because it cost God the life of his Son: "ye were bought at a price," and what has cost God much cannot be cheap for us. Above all, it is *grace* because God did not reckon his Son too dear a price to pay for our life, but delivered him up for us. Costly grace is the Incarnation of God.

DIETRICH BONHOEFFER

GERMANY (1906–1945)

*G*ive us grace, O God, to dare to do the deed which we well know cries to be done. Let us not hesitate because of ease, or the words of men's mouths, or our own lives. Mighty causes are calling us—the freeing of women, the training of children, the putting down of hate and murder and poverty—all these and more. But they call with voices that mean work and sacrifice and death. Mercifully grant us, O God, the spirit of Esther, that we say: I will go unto the King and if I perish, I perish—Amen.

W. E. B. DUBOIS
UNITED STATES (1868–1963)

35

*C*hrist's bursting forth from the tomb on Easter was a howling wind, but it did not uproot the tree of the cross.

ROBERT SMITH
UNITES STATES

CHAPTER 4

Growth Through Loss

(Jesus Meets His Mother)

*T*aking up the cross can present a challenge to our most precious relationships. Picture Christ meeting his mother on the path to Calvary. Each had made life-changing choices—hers, many years before, to risk public humiliation in assenting to the angel Gabriel's announcement; his, to live out his awakening to God's call. There they stand on that Friday in Jerusalem, profoundly aware that their choices have taken them on twisting journeys, propelling them out of the predictable and safe associations of village life into unfamiliar, sometimes hostile, territory, and have turned their relationships upside down. From maiden, mother, and refugee, to the pierced heart of maternal grief. From boy in Torah class and carpenter's apprentice to prophet, healer, teacher, and criminal.

We too are often faced with decisions that entail the unpredictable, the unknown, the difficult. These can seem disconcertingly like a death, like

Calvary, which Joyce Rupp describes in this chapter as "the deepest good-bye that anyone has ever known." Opening before us lies a chasm of change—leaving behind a way of life, a familiar pattern, a spent relationship; letting go of our possessiveness of others, our anxieties, our superficial self, our fear of death.

Only our abandonment to God will sustain us throughout what Maggie Ross calls the "major dislocations and new beginnings" and the "small deaths" that each letting go entails.

Through the growth of self-offering, however, we come to see that courageous surrenders build new communities, open new paths, and bring forth life and liberation. These writers, like Carter Heyward, encourage us to see that "the losing and the finding are a single process."

*W*e are changed . . . by the eucharistic offering of each life, by lives and deaths around us, by lives and deaths in our own lives, not only major dislocations and new beginnings, but also small deaths, our hurting of each other and forgiving of each other. Having passed through death and resurrection, we are expelled into the world to transfigure with God's infinitely expanding love.

. . . We still have to choose: to listen to the fantasies that ravel deeper into anger, resentment, and hate, or to change and grow . . . wrestling with the God whom we will not let go, and who will not let us go until we receive the fire from heaven that makes us a sacrifice for creation's healing, blessing, and joy.

MAGGIE ROSS
UNITED STATES

*I*t is abundantly clear that *this* lifetime is a series of simultaneous deaths and births. . . . It is also clear that the farther one travels on the journey of life, the more births one will experience, and therefore the more deaths—the more joy and the more pain.

M. SCOTT PECK
UNITED STATES

*E*very acceptance of suffering is an acceptance of that which exists. The denial of every form of suffering can result in a flight from reality in which contact with reality becomes ever thinner, ever more fragmentary. It is impossible to remove oneself totally from suffering, unless one removes oneself from life itself, no longer enters into relationships, makes oneself invulnerable. Contrary to what one might wish, pain, losses, amputations are part of even the smoothest life one can imagine—separation from parents, the fading of childhood friendships, the death of certain people who had become especially important in our lives, growing old, the dying of relatives and friends, finally death. The more strongly we affirm reality, the more we are immersed in it, the more deeply we are touched by these processes of dying which surround us and press in upon us.

DOROTHEE SÖLLE

GERMANY

*T*hroughout our lives, death and birth repeat themselves. Many little deaths lead to many little births. We die to wombs and are born into worlds. But these worlds become larger wombs for us. We die to them and are born into larger worlds: our mother's womb, the breast, the nursery, the home, neighborhood, family, school, each grade in school, friends, jobs, cities. We are like multistage rockets; each stage dies and falls away when its job is done, for its job is only to launch us forward.

PETER KREEFT

UNITED STATES

We turn back to God and ask for his strength to renounce, not our suffering, not our pain, not a particular cross, but the tight hold we have on the leaves of the self.

JUDITH C. LECHMAN
UNITED STATES

*J*esus has passed through death to new life, but the vowed followers of Jesus have to be urged to move on from the tomb and from the past. It was, after all, a past in which they could always depend on him and leave everything to him to do. It seemed a safe past; they may have resented the way he moved on to death and beyond to new life. His moving on presented them with a crisis, a call for commitment in a much deeper way, a call for their death to their old life, even of dependence on Jesus to handle every situation.

MONIKA K. HELLWIG
UNITED STATES

*A*t the center of Christian faith is a curious paradox: if we are to save our lives, we must lose them. If we are to live as whole people, we must be broken. If we are to know peace, we must enter into conflict. If we are to be certain about anything, we must be able to celebrate the ambiguities within us and around us. If we are to ascend into heaven, we must descend into hell.

For years, I envisioned losing and finding one's life as being not only distinctly separate experiences, but also as best accessible to me in chronological order: I must first live in doubt and conflict. I might later grow into faith and peace. Metaphorically, I must first be crucified; I might someday know the glory of the resurrection.

Gradually, I began to realize that life does not exist for me somewhere further down the pike. We do not become whole people, saved people, peaceful people the day we finish therapy, give our lives to Christ, get married, get ordained, or set ourselves in some new direction. Again and again we are aware of our wholeness and our salvation when we are able to face and enter into the brokenness and confusion within us, between us in relationship, and around us in the world. In paradox the contradictions are concurrent. We do not lose life today and "win" it tomorrow, as a reward for having died. The losing and the finding are a single process, a single reality. I live and I die simultaneously. I am faithful and doubtful at the same time. If I know who I am today, and I do, it is in the knowing of myself as a person who, like anyone, does not know much at all about who she is.

CARTER HEYWARD
UNITED STATES

*J*esus, in his weak, broken, helpless condition, "cried out in a loud voice: 'My God, My God, why have you deserted me?'" (Mt. 27:46). This cry of the beloved Son is the cry of every person who has known a devastating goodbye in his or her life, when the overpowering feeling of aloneness, emptiness, desolation, abandonment, fills the human spirit. . . .

If we were left with Jesus' emptiness and desolation, if we had only our kinship with him in his goodbyes, it would not be enough to sustain us in our own leave-taking. We would draw comfort, but we would not have the hope of a future hello. The beauty of the paschal mystery, the mystery of passing over from death to life, of moving from goodbye to hello, is that it ends with hello. If Calvary is the deepest goodbye that anyone has ever known, then the resurrection is the greatest hello that anyone has ever proclaimed.

. . . Jesus risen is a proclamation of "hello." He is a witness to us that when goodbyes do come that we can grow through them. We can be changed, transformed. We can be raised from our empty places of loss and can experience something new within us.

JOYCE RUPP, O.S.M.

UNITED STATES

CHAPTER 5

Costly Involvement

(The Cross Is Laid on Simon of Cyrene)

*W*hen Simon of Cyrene enters the drama of Jesus' ascent to Golgotha, he appears as an unsuspecting onlooker coerced into carrying the cross for Jesus. But as the church began to tell the story of that episode in Christ's passion, it emphasized not Simon's unwitting involvement, but his symbolic action. He exemplified for believers an active, not passive, choice to become involved with Christ and thus with others. In more recent times, Simon has become the patron saint of people who work among outcasts.

Taking action on behalf of others may put us at risk personally and sometimes politically. I may see those "whose hands I do not want to touch"; nevertheless they are my responsibility. I may suffer physical pain, rejection, and even terrorism, but my commitment to the greater cause—

to overcoming estrangement and to ensuring just and merciful relation-ships—compels me to endure.

Once we know our own brokenness, embrace the cross, and realize Christ's desire to mend, we are obligated then to heal others' wounds and the wounds of creation. Action faithful to Simon of Cyrene's model may take the form of a seemingly unremarkable late-night watch with a friend in trouble. It may be patient listening to a neglected child. It may involve a commitment to a simpler, more sensitive lifestyle that entails deliberate, real, and holy deprivation and inconvenience. It may mean storming the halls of government. Taking action on behalf of others is the evidence that Christ's followers have truly understood his passion and share it with him by the testimony of their works.

*J*esus has gone ahead of us on the journey, but not instead of us.

LARRY L. RASMUSSEN
UNITED STATES

*I*nvolvement in any action takes an effort, and there is always a price to pay. The question is, am I ready to pay the price, to share the suffering of others? Suffering for me is bearable, if it is for the cause of liberation, if it helps us to find a new community with each other and with God.

JEAN ZARU
OCCUPIED WEST BANK (RAMALLAH)

O God:
Enlarge my heart
that it may be big enough to receive the greatness of your
   love.
Stretch my heart
that it may take into it all those who with me around the
   world
believe in Jesus Christ.
Stretch it
that it may take into it all those who do not know him,
but who are my responsibility because I know him.
And stretch it
that it may take in all those who are not lovely in my eyes,
and whose hands I do not want to touch;
through Jesus Christ, my savior, Amen.

PRAYER OF AN AFRICAN CHRISTIAN

We must say to our white brothers all over the South who try to keep us down: We will match your capacity to inflict suffering with our capacity to endure suffering. We will meet your physical force with soul force. We will not hate you. And yet we cannot in all good conscience obey your evil laws. Do to us what you will. Threaten our children and we will still love you, . . . Say that we're too low, that we're too degraded, yet we will still love you. Bomb our homes and go by our churches early in the morning and bomb them if you please, and we will still love you. We will wear you down by our capacity to suffer. In winning the victory we will not only win our freedom. We will so appeal to your heart and your conscience that we will win you in the process.

MARTIN LUTHER KING, JR.
UNITED STATES (1929–1968)

*W*e all bleed.
We bleed for ourselves—we each
have our private pain.
We bleed for others;
and we bleed for a wounded world.
If we did not bleed for others at some
times and in some measure,
would we not be spiritually barren?
Unfit for our calling.
Incapable of conceiving and nurturing
new life,
in forming relationships and caring
communities.
But if the pain takes over, the bleeding becomes
constant.
Do we not then find that we have
lost touch with our Lord—
He is obscured by the crowd of our
concerns—the crowd of our activities—

perhaps even the crowd of our own
words.
Jesus, help us to touch you now,
to lay before you our own, and the
world's pain.
Help us as we wait in silence
to feel your hands upon us.

CONSULTATION OF
METHODIST WOMEN MINISTERS

*L*ike Jesus, he who proclaims liberation is called not only to care
for his own wounds and the wounds of others, but also to
make his wounds into a major source of his healing power.

HENRI NOUWEN
UNITED STATES

*T*he Christian
must have the courage
to follow Christ.
The Christian
who is risen in Christ
must dare
to be like Christ:
he must dare to follow conscience
even in unpopular causes.
He must, if necessary,
be able to disagree with the majority
and make decisions
that he knows
to be according to the Gospel
and teaching of Christ,
even when others
do not understand
why he is acting this way.

THOMAS MERTON
UNITED STATES (1915–1968)

*B*oth Jesus and his great disciple [Paul] accepted the wound in the creation, and having accepted it, devoted their lives to the healing of it.

That is the creative act, not to ask who dealt this wound to the creation, not to accuse God of having dealt it, but to make of one's life an instrument of God's peace. This act is doubly creative, in that it transforms both giver and receiver, and indeed it can be said of many of us that one of our deepest experiences of God is in this act of giving and receiving.

ALAN PATON

SOUTH AFRICA (1903–1988)

I spent [one Easter] at L'Arche community at Trosly Breuil outside Paris. It was there, as an outsider to the community, that I saw more clearly than ever before the prophetic nature of caring for those who are, in economic terms, useless. It is a lavishing of precious resources, our precious ointment on the handicapped, the insane, the rejected and the dying that most clearly reveals the love of Christ in our times. It is this gratuitous caring, this unilateral declaration of love which proclaims the gospel more powerfully than bishops and theologians. It is an ongoing reenactment of the drama at the house at Bethany, when Mary took the alabaster box of ointment, of "Spikenard very precious," and poured it over Jesus' head. I wonder sometimes if either Mary or Jesus was aware of the full significance of this outrageous public gesture of love. Perhaps, like today's carers, they acted instinctively from their true centers, recognizing a need and moving out to meet it, whatever the price, whatever the consequences.

SHEILA CASSIDY

ENGLAND

*H*eavenly Father, whose blessed Son came not to be served but to serve: Bless all who, following in his steps, give themselves to the service of others; that with wisdom, patience, and courage, they may minister in his Name to the suffering, the friendless, and the needy; for the love of him who laid down his life for us, your Son our Savior Jesus Christ, who lives and reigns with you and the Holy Spirit, one God, for ever and ever. *Amen.*

BOOK OF COMMON PRAYER

CHAPTER 6

Seeing Christ in Others

(A Woman Wipes the Face of Jesus)

As Jesus made his way toward Golgotha, a woman stepped out from the crowd. Picture this woman—perhaps a secret follower of Jesus. He staggers toward her, sweat stinging his eyes, blood trickling down his cheek. She would have been moved with compassion for Jesus, but she might have also wondered to herself: "What can I do? He's going to be crucified. And I'm a woman. I might end up in trouble with the authorities; my family might suffer. And for what? His fate is sealed. My best bet is to hide in the crowd . . . I can feel sorry for him . . . maybe say a prayer for him . . . "

But this compassionate, courageous woman stepped out and did what she could. She wiped the face of Jesus. Her action, small as it may seem, sets a precedent for us. Often we feel overwhelmed by needs around us. We want to flip past the picture of the hungry child, or buy new curtains to distract ourselves from the needs of the homeless, or give quick-fix advice to those who are hurting. The action of this woman and the voices in this chapter challenge us not to withdraw, not to pull away from involvement, but instead to see Jesus and seize the opportunity to do the sacrificial (and often unstrategic) act.

Moved by the face of Christ in others, we step out of the crowd. But as we step out, we find we are not alone. We are gathered there, with the women who stood by the cross and with others of past centuries who have been willing to stand apart to follow Jesus. We find ourselves in fellowship with those of our own time who suffer for Jesus' sake. We come to see Jesus even in those whom we had learned to fear or despise. We, like Mother Teresa, may find ourselves unified with those who suffer as we "see Christ in the bruised body and the dirty rags." We find strength in these fellow travelers, learning that in our community, when some are too weak to pray, others may carry them.

As we see Christ in others, we realize that as long as people are suffering, Jesus is in agony. We must not sleep, but watch and act.

*T*o watch with Jesus, not to fall asleep during the time of his fear of death, which lasts till the end of the world and has in view all the fearful, is an ancient Christian demand that is contrary to every natural response to affliction.

DOROTHEE SÖLLE

GERMANY

*A*ll through those weary first days in jail when I was in solitary confinement, the only thoughts that brought comfort to my soul were those lines in the Psalms that expressed the terror and misery of man suddenly stricken and abandoned. Solitude and hunger and weariness of spirit—these sharpened my perceptions so that I suffered not only my own sorrow but the sorrows of those about me. I was no longer myself. I was man. I was no longer a young girl, part of a radical movement seeking justice for those oppressed. I was the oppressed. I was that drug addict, screaming and tossing in her cell, beating her head against the wall. I was that shoplifter who for rebellion was sentenced to solitary. I was that woman who had killed her children, who had murdered her lover.

The blackness of hell was all about me. The sorrows of the world encompassed me. I was like one gone down into the pit. Hope had forsaken me. I was that mother whose child had been raped and slain. I was the mother who had borne the monster who had done it. I was even that monster, feeling in my own heart every abomination.

DOROTHY DAY
UNITED STATES (1897–1980)

62

When we are dealing with the sick, we are touching the body of Christ who suffers. This contact gives us a heroism that makes us forget all disgust.

We need a deep faith in order to see Christ in the bruised body and the dirty rags. Under them is hidden the one who is fairer in beauty than the sons of men. We need the hands of Christ in order to touch those bodies wounded by suffering.

MOTHER TERESA
INDIA (1910–1997)

I was in an underground train, a crowded train in which all sorts of people jostled together, sitting and strap hanging—workers of every description going home at the end of the day. Quite suddenly I saw with my mind, but as vividly as a wonderful picture, Christ in them all. But I saw more than that; not only was Christ in every one of them, being in them, dying in them, rejoicing in them, sorrowing in them—but because He was in them, and because they were here, the whole world was here too in this underground train, not only the world as it was at that moment, not only all the people in all the countries of the world, but all those people who have lived in the past and all those yet to come.

I came out into the street and walked for a long time in the crowds. It was the same here on every side, in every passer-by, everywhere—Christ.

. . . I saw too the reverence that everyone must have for a sinner; instead of condoning his sin, which is in reality his utmost sorrow, one must comfort Christ who is suffering in him. And this reverence must be paid even to those sinners whose souls seem to be dead, because it is Christ, who is the life of the soul, who is dead in them: they are His tombs, and Christ in the tomb is potentially the risen Christ.

CARYLL HOUSELANDER
ENGLAND (1901–1954)

*T*he world has shrunk. The capsizing of a ferry boat in the Philippines, or the strife between different ethnic groups in Sri Lanka, now makes front-page headlines. We are literally drowning in news of suffering from all around the globe. We cannot help being affected by it. How much more, then, those who have deliberately opened their hearts to the creation as one family in God?

We humans are far too frail and tiny to bear all that pain. The solution is not avoidance, however. Not reading or listening to the news is no protection; I am convinced that our solidarity with all of life is somatic, and that we sense the universal suffering whether we wish to or not.

What we need is a portable form of the Wailing Wall in Jerusalem, where we can unburden ourselves of this accumulated suffering. We *need* to experience it; it is a part of reality. Our task in praying is precisely that of giving speech to the Spirit's groanings within us. But we must not try to bear the sufferings of the creation ourselves.

We are to articulate these agonizing longings and let them pass through us to God. Only the heart of the loving God can endure such a weight of suffering. Our attempts to bear them (and our depression is evidence that we try) are masochistic, falsely messianic, and finally idolatrous, as if there were no God, as if we had to carry this burden all by ourselves.

WALTER WINK
UNITED STATES

*M*y own heart's blood,
My Christ on the cross,
Where are you, where have they laid you?
Are you under arrest or under the soil?
God let you be in my womb
and I carried you nine long months;
they snatched you from my womb
and me they abandoned maimed.
The way of the Cross,
of Herod or Pilate
is the way of cruelty
and the washing of hands.
But the way they thought
to be ending in Calvary
dissolved in resurrection,
in a shroud and an empty tomb.

The way of my cross
through prisons and processes
takes me nowhere
except to the Plaza de Mayo.
Passer-by, unheeding and silently unaware:
tell me if there be any grief

as great as a bodiless burial.
Tell me and do not pass by—
Nor wash your hands!
Do not forget there are other Christs,
the victims of new crucifixions!
And Mary, his mother, is weeping again
in the Plaza de Mayo.

ANONYMOUS
ARGENTINA, 1980s

*D*istancing ourselves from each other's pain is the hidden agenda behind most of our efforts to "fix" each other with advice. If you take my advice, and do it right, you will get well and I will be off the hook. But if you do not follow my advice, or do not follow it properly, I am off the hook nonetheless: I have done the best I could, and your continued suffering is clearly your fault. By trying to fix you with advice, rather than simply suffering with you, I hold myself away from your pain.

PARKER PALMER
UNITED STATES

*J*esus was willing to endure pain so others could live with less pain. He was willing to suffer gossip so a woman could experience acceptance. He was willing to suffer betrayal so Judas could have friendship. He was willing to suffer ultimate rejection, even rejection from his own religious tradition, so others could have his word.

Service costs. The servant suffers. There is the preoccupying agony of caring until it hurts. The sacrifice of time. The struggle to talk when every word aches. And no guarantees. Suffering servanthood is only for those who take following seriously. It is for those who can carry others because they have first carried themselves.

FRAN FERDER
UNITED STATES

O Lord our God,
we thank you for the many people throughout the ages
who have followed your way of life joyfully:
for the many saints and martyrs, men and women,
who have offered up their very lives,
so that your life abundant may become manifest.
For your love and faithfulness we will at all times praise you.

O Lord, we thank you for those who chose the way of Jesus
Christ.
In the midst of trial, they held out hope;
in the midst of hatred, they kindled love;
in the midst of persecutions, they witnessed to your power;
in the midst of despair, they clung to your promise.
For your love and faithfulness we will at all times praise you.

O Lord, we thank you for the truth they passed on to us: that
it is by giving that we shall receive;
it is by becoming weak that we shall be strong;
it is by loving others that we shall be loved;

it is by offering ourselves that the kingdom will unfold;
it is by dying that we shall inherit life everlasting.

Lord give us courage to follow your way of life.
For your love and faithfulness we will at all times praise you.

NATIONAL COUNCIL OF CHURCHES
OF THE PHILIPPINES

*T*he Gospel stories record images of a strong collective of women. The phrase "a group of women" appears many times in the Jesus narratives. The strongest evidence of this group was at the foot of the cross. The women stood in solidarity with each other in a situation that must have been frightening and bewildering to them. Their collective support empowered them to keep going when there seemed to be no hope. Later, when the disciples refused to believe Mary's report of her encounter with the risen Christ, a group of women went back to the empty tomb. Women believing in women.

RANJINI REBERA
SRI LANKA/AUSTRALIA

One of the powers of faith community is its capacity to provide a lasting steadiness through all the waverings of its individual members. When I cannot pray, the prayer of countless others goes on. Where I am complacent, others are struggling. Where I am in conflict, others are at peace. Most important, when I cannot act in loving ways, there are those in my communities who can.

GERALD MAY
UNITED STATES

CHAPTER 7

Divine Weakness

(Jesus Falls a Second Time)

Tradition has it that during the Way of the Cross, Jesus fell a total of three times. We are clearly reminded that Jesus was entirely human and felt the full weight of the cross. Here, as he falls a second time, we are invited to meditate on the implications of Christ's, and by extension God's, weakness.

The cross shatters the image of God as almighty but impervious and impassive. In Jesus' crucifixion we see a God of vulnerability and humility. This is the God who can suffer with humanity, whose self-giving extends even to enduring death. Such a notion seems utterly foolish, even unnatural. Omniscient, omnipotent, immortal, invisible—we understand those divine attributes; they seem to fit comfortably. But a self-giving, self-emptying, flesh-baring God?

In the cross—this scandal of reversals—we are compelled to refocus our vision of God from the lofty realms of heavenly safety to the dirt-stained face of Christ. This new vision leads us to question the likening of God to some of our culture's ideals: the "tearless male" or the rich and powerful ruler. God's self-disclosure on the cross, a self with a capacity to suffer and to be exposed, may help us, as it did Nicholas Wolterstorff, to see God in "the face of that woman with soup tin in hand and bloated child at side."

*N*ormally we begin at a beginning; we start with creation. God the all-powerful fashions the universe in a flurry of divine creativity. But because creation tumbles into sin, God shows up with tablets of law to be tossed down from Mount Sinai. Usually we begin by presuming a God of unlimited power, a law-and-order God whose control is absolute. . . . Normally we do theology by introducing a big-bang God almighty from the start.

Then we flip to the Christian scriptures and start chattering about redemption. God almighty, a holy terror, relents. God unclenches the divine fist and lets a little heart show through at the cross; as a result, we are "saved by the blood," as they say. Because we are properly committed to substitutionary atonement, we end up with God's love sacrificing Jesus, who is God-with-us, to God's justice in order to redeem a fouled-up creation. Our usual sequence is to begin with creation, an enterprise that demonstrates the absolute power of God, and then to introduce redemption as a moderating of God's power with something we tend to label "love."

But suppose we start with the cross and work ourselves back to creation. What then? Suppose we begin, as does Paul, with the foolish weakness of the cross. Yes, obviously the universe is an awesome display of power; a big-bang God has been at work. But what *kind* of power is God's power? Perhaps God's power is the modest power of a God willing to shatter divine perfections in order to give life. Perhaps creation is not so much an act of masculine domination as of self-giving, something like the agony of childbirth. And suppose the founding of the law on Sinai is not so much strong-armed police action or judicial regulation as a motherly kindness that seeks to offer freedom within protective guidance. . . .

Do you see now how the cross redefines our doctrines of God? . . . God's attributes—omnipotence, omniscience, omnipresence, perfection—are all redefined by the broken body of the crucified Christ. God's self-abnegating love, a willing-to-die love, is written across all time and space. . . . Here is God who all along has been willing to be impotent, to not know, to suffer with, to die for a people, a dearly loved people. Here is a God whose real name, long hidden from our minds, is Compassion (*com pati* = to suffer with).

DAVID BUTTRICK
UNITED STATES

*N*atural humanity did not and could not have imagined that suffering rather than power might be a mode of being for God. To know God from the standpoint of the cross is to abide with God in his passion.

JON SOBRINO
EL SALVADOR

*O*ne early drawing showed Christ crucified with the head of an ass, so absurd was the notion of a crucified God seen by intelligent people. It was, as Paul said, foolishness (1 Corinthians 1:23), yet the early Christians saw it as "the foolishness of God" (1:25). Through this act of foolishness, they claimed, salvation had come to the world.

KENNETH LEECH
ENGLAND

*T*he passion of Christ is a manifestation of the nature and activity of God, but it is bewilderingly difficult for us to grasp. All our models of power and authority are useless when it comes to understanding the power of God, except by way of complete reversal. . . . The picture we have of the kingship of Christ in the gospels is a heart-breaking cartoon. We do not see him leading armies or holding forth to great assemblies or receiving the homage of princes. We see him torn, bloody and helpless, nailed to a cross. We see him so helpless he cannot brush away the flies that cling to his wounds or wipe away the blood that runs down his face. There can be no greater helplessness than the experience of hanging on a cross.

RICHARD HOLLOWAY

SCOTLAND

*G*od is not only the God of the sufferers but the God who suffers. The pain and fallenness of humanity have entered into his heart. Through the prism of my tears I have seen a suffering God.

It is said of God that no one can behold his face and live. I always thought this meant that no one could see his splendor and live. A friend said perhaps it meant that no one could see his sorrow and live. Or perhaps his sorrow is splendor.

And great mystery: to redeem our brokenness and lovelessness the God who suffers with us did not strike some mighty blow of power but sent his beloved son to suffer *like* us, through his suffering to redeem us from suffering and evil.

Instead of explaining our suffering, God shares it. But I never saw it. Though I confessed that the man of sorrows was God himself, I never saw the God of sorrows. Though I confessed that the man bleeding on the cross was the redeeming God, I never saw God himself on the cross, blood from sword and thorn and nail dripping healing into the world's wounds.

What does this mean for life, that God suffers? I'm only beginning to learn. When we think of God the Creator, then we naturally see the rich and powerful of the earth as his closest image. But when we hold steady before us the sight of God the Redeemer redeeming from sin and suffering by suffering, then perhaps we must look elsewhere for earth's closest icon. Where? Perhaps to the face of that woman with soup tin in hand and bloated child at side. Perhaps that is why Jesus said that inasmuch as we show love to such a one, we show love to him.

NICHOLAS WOLTERSTORFF

UNITED STATES

To consider the tearless male as an ideal is to acknowledge clearly that nothing is learned from suffering and nothing to be gained from it.

DOROTHEE SÖLLE

GERMANY

*B*ut the servant-form was no mere outer garment, and therefore God must suffer all things, endure all things, make experience of all things. He must suffer hunger in the desert, he must thirst in the time of his agony, he must be forsaken in death, *absolutely like the humblest*—behold the man! His suffering is not that of his death, but this entire life is a story of suffering; and it is love that suffers, the love which gives all is itself in want.

SØREN KIERKEGAARD
DENMARK (1813–1855)

*W*hen the crucified Jesus is called the "image of the invisible God," the meaning is that *this* is God, and God is like *this*. God is not greater than he is in this humiliation. God is not more glorious than he is in this self-surrender. God is not more powerful than he is in this helplessness. God is not more divine than he is in this humanity.

JÜRGEN MOLTMANN

GERMANY

*G*od's death cannot be contained in our thoughts; instead, it tears them apart. For God is Life, and Christ called Himself Life, and yet . . . there is Life in the tomb. "O Life, how can it be that you have died?" In Christ's death we bow down before the ultimate mystery of the Incarnation, of the sacrificial self-emptying of Godhood; this is indeed the power of God's love for man.

SERGEI NIKOLAEVICH BULGAKOV
RUSSIA / UNITED STATES (1871–1944)

CHAPTER 8

Compassion

(Jesus Meets the Women of Jerusalem)

"*D*aughters of Jerusalem," Jesus said under the weight of his cross, "do not weep for me; no, weep for yourselves and for your children." In the midst of his own pain, Jesus felt even more sharply the agony yet to befall these women of Jerusalem. Pity more yourselves—your calamities and trauma—than me.

Jesus' sympathy for these women is expressed only in the Gospel of Luke. Compiling his story in the aftermath of the Roman army's destruction of Jerusalem in 70, Luke could still hear the weeping of the war's victims. Some forty years after Jesus walked the path to Golgotha, Luke felt the heart of Jesus split not from his own pain, but from these women's. Jesus' words to the women of Jerusalem became a treasured reassurance of his compassion for the generation that followed.

The daughters of Jerusalem in Luke's time indeed experienced disaster and agony. They saw Roman soldiers slaughter their neighbors. They were besieged. They starved to death and watched helplessly as their children perished.

Your pain will be greater than mine, Jesus laments. This is the Jesus we recognize, the one who for the three years of his ministry had been propelled by just such compassion. The selections that follow honor divine compassion and Christ's fellow feeling with us. Like the God whom the Psalms extol as the tender and compassionate helper, Jesus is acquainted with our grief and understands our predicament. He "is also displaced" and has "become an exile with us," say displaced *campesinos* from Peru. A former slave relates her agonies and derives comfort only from the listening Jesus.

In our needs and emptiness, we cling to this foundational truth: The divine nature radiates sympathy with us, desires to share our pain, and identifies with our condition.

*W*hatever God does, the first outburst is always compassion.

MEISTER ECKHART
GERMANY (1260–1329)

*J*esus,
You have heard our tears:
the tears women have shed in silence
because we were afraid to be heard;
the tears women have held back
thinking we deserved violence;
the tears we have not held back
but were not comforted;
the tears women have wept alone
because we would not ask to be held;
the tears women weep together
because our sisters cannot feed their children;
because our sisters live in fear;
because the earth herself is threatened.

So we weep.

JANET MORLEY
ENGLAND

*W*hat is a compassionate heart? It is a kindling of the heart for all creation—for mankind, the birds, the animals, even the enemies of the truth and for all that is. And when he thinks of them or contemplates them, tears stream from his eyes because of the power of mercy which moves his heart with great compassion. And the heart feels itself touched, and he cannot endure to see or hear a creature suffer any harm, even the slightest pain. And he offers then, even for those who hurt him, continuous prayers and tears, that they might be saved and strengthened. Even for those that creep in the dust does he pray—out of the immense compassion which is poured out into his heart without measure, following the example of God.

ISAAC THE SYRIAN
(LATE SEVENTH CENTURY)

O Lord, Jesus Christ, Who art as the Shadow of a Great Rock in a weary land, Who beholdest Thy weak creatures weary of labour, weary of pleasure, weary of hope deferred, weary of self; in Thine abundant compassion, and fellow-feeling with us, and unutterable tenderness, bring us, we pray Thee, unto Thy rest
. . . Amen.

CHRISTINA ROSSETTI
ENGLAND (1830–1894)

*J*esus is the one place in the world where we need not restrain our sorrows because He already knows them all.

HELMUT THIELICKE
GERMANY (1908–1985)

*E*verything that happens to the individual Christian, . . . such as the terrors of sin, anxiety and grief of the heart, torture, or death, He regards as though it happened to Him.

MARTIN LUTHER
GERMANY (1483–1546)

*D*at man ober dar say dat women needs to be helped into carriages, and lifted ober ditches, and to have de best place every whar. Nobody eber help me into carriages, or ober mud puddles, or gives me any best place [and raising herself to her full height and her voice to a pitch like rolling thunder, she asked], and ar'n't I a woman? Look at me! Look at my arm! [And she bared her right arm to the shoulder, showing her tremendous muscular power.] I have plowed, and planted, and gathered into barns, and no man could head me—and ar'n't I a woman? I could work as much and eat as much as a man (when I could get it), and bear de lash as well—and ar'n't I a woman? I have borne thirteen chilern and seen 'em mos' all sold off into slavery, and when I cried out with a mother's grief, none but Jesus heard—and ar'n't I a woman?

SOJOURNER TRUTH
UNITED STATES (1797–1883)

God, our promised land;
Christ, our way,
our journey has become long and hard
because we wander about
like nomads
not knowing where to go.
We are strangers in our own land,
without bread, a roof, a future.
But you came to find us
with your life-giving breath,
You, who are also displaced,
have become an exile with us.
You offer us anew the promised land. Your spirit urges us
    toward that joyous homecoming.

DISPLACED *CAMPESINOS*

PERU, 1980s

CHAPTER 9

Kept in Hope
(Jesus Falls a Third Time)

*M*ost of us would like to believe that we can control our lives and postpone (almost indefinitely) our deaths. This fallacy may be easier for many of us living today to believe: we can order the model with air bags, request the full battery of medical tests, and eat health food. But when we consider Jesus on his way to Golgotha, we know that control is a mirage.

The writers in this chapter have seen this illusion for what it is, perhaps so clearly because they lived in an era of uncertainty, or because they have been desperately poor, or because they are being terrorized by an oppressive regime.

If we cannot control our lives, what comfort is there? Jesus, his journey nearly over, falls again under the weight of his burden. His strength is waning. How outrageous for a passerby to have said to Jesus as he lay there, "Hey, don't worry . . . be happy . . . it will all work out." Yet this is precisely the tone of the cheap "comfort" the bereaved and dying are sometimes offered: "You'll see them in heaven!" "Why don't you just have another baby?" These are the easy answers.

Our fellow pilgrims on this journey don't offer the easy comfort of denial or analgesia. On the contrary, they affirm what we know—that life is unpredictable, difficult, and challenging.

We don't need voices to tell us that nothing will go wrong, or that we deserve compensation if it does. These writers give us what we need: a new perspective. They assure us that, despite the chaos of our worst calamity, we need not fear. Although control is an illusion, and "the things that you are afraid of are quite likely to happen," as John Macmurray reminds us in this chapter, we will not be overcome. These are those who have emerged from trauma, hopeful because they have sensed the nurturing, comforting love of God; they are at peace because of God's faithfulness.

Even Jesus fell under the weight of his cross. But these voices assure us that as we face the darkness, we begin to find a secure hope, an unshakable foundation. Like Jesus, we are offered not a way out of, but a way through the darkness, and, as Dorothee Sölle says, the "cup of suffering becomes the cup of strengthening."

*A*ll extreme suffering evokes the experience of being forsaken by God. In the depth of suffering people see themselves as abandoned and forsaken by everyone.

. . . The ground on which life was built, the primal trust in the world's reliability—a reliability conveyed in many diverse ways—is destroyed.

The experience that Jesus had in Gethsemane goes beyond this destruction. It is the experience of assent. The cup of suffering becomes the cup of strengthening. Whoever empties that cup has conquered all fear. The one who at the end returns from prayer to the sleeping disciples is a different person from the one who went off to pray. He is clear-eyed and awake; he trembles no longer. "It is enough: the hour has come. Rise, let us be going." An angel came down to Jesus no more than one comes down to other people—or no less than that! Both perspectives are true: Mark and Luke are only using varied ways of putting the matter. One can say that in every prayer an angel waits for us, since every prayer changes the one who prays, strengthens him, in that it pulls him together and brings him to the utmost attention, which in suffering is forced from us and which in loving we ourselves give.

DOROTHEE SÖLLE
GERMANY

All religion is concerned to overcome fear. . . . The maxim of illusory religion runs: "Fear not; trust in God and He will see that none of the things you fear will happen to you." That of real religion, on the contrary, is, "Fear not; the things that you are afraid of are quite likely to happen to you, but they are nothing to be afraid of."

JOHN MACMURRAY
SCOTLAND (1891–1976)

*M*any people suffer because of the false supposition on which they have based their lives. That supposition is that there should be no fear or loneliness, no confusion or doubt. But these sufferings can only be dealt with creatively when they are understood as wounds integral to our human condition. Therefore ministry is a very *confronting* service. It does not allow people to live with illusions of immortality and wholeness. It keeps reminding others that they are mortal and broken, but also that with the recognition of this condition, liberation starts.

HENRI NOUWEN
UNITED STATES

*R*emember that young woman I saw that day, bleeding from her womb, clutching herself where they had speared her, sobbing that she would lose the baby that was growing inside her? Here again is a story of life coming where there should be death. This is the story—finally—of the child called Hope. The woman bled and bled as the assassins rampaged through my church; they had knifed her where they knew it would do the most damage. These are men who see a mother and want to damage what is within her. Insanity. Somehow, the woman, bleeding and sobbing, was brought to a hospital.

Everyone in Port-au-Prince had heard the story of the godless attack against the young mother and her unborn child. And the criminals, that night, after the massacre had ended, went to the university hospital, searching the maternity wards. They had heard that the woman had survived, and they wanted to kill her, to show the people that there was no hope in this world. They made the mothers in the maternity ward lift their white nightgowns to see if they were wounded in the stomach. Indecency. But they never found the woman. She had been taken to another hospital far away, and there—miracle, miracle—she was delivered, by caesarean, of a baby girl, a wounded baby girl, but fine, healthy, more or less undamaged. And that child she called Esperancia, or Hope. Because the baby's birth showed that the murderers, the assassins, the criminals, the police, the Army, the president and all the president's men could not put an end to Hope in Haiti, could not destroy us, could not wreck our infant aspirations with their knives and spears. Hope's birth showed that a new Haiti could emerge from the wounded body of the old, that in spite of the atrocities visited upon Haiti, she could give forth new life, if only her friends would help her, and shelter her, and protect her, and help her with the birth. Hope is the new generation of my country.

JEAN-BERTRAND ARISTIDE

HAITI

*G*entle nurse, gentle mother, who are these sons to whom you give birth and nurture if not those whom you bear and educate in the faith of Christ by your teaching? . . . For, as that blessed faith is born and nurtured in us by the other apostles also, how much more by you, because you have labored and accomplished more in this than all the others. . . . O mother of well known tenderness, may your son feel your heart of maternal piety. . . .

But you, Jesus, good lord, are you not also a mother? Are you not that mother who, like a hen, collects her chickens under her wings? Truly, master, you are a mother. For what others have conceived and given birth to, they have received from you.

. . . You are the author, others are the ministers. It is then you, above all, Lord God, who are mother.

Christ, mother, who gathers under your wings your little ones, your dead chick seeks refuge under your wings. For by your gentleness, those who are hurt are comforted; by your perfume, the despairing are reformed. Your warmth resuscitates the dead; your touch justifies sinners. . . . Console your chicken, resuscitate your dead one, justify your sinner. May your injured one be consoled by you; may he who of himself despairs be comforted by you and re-formed through you in your complete and unceasing grace. For the consolation of the wretched flows from you, blessed, world without end, Amen.

ANSELM OF CANTERBURY
ENGLAND (C. 1033–1109)

We have gone through circumstances of great privation, anxiety and suffering. All these seemed at times to weaken our sense of dependence on God. But when I know that wherever I am, whether in affluence or in poverty, whether I have personal liberty or not, God has a service for me to render, I feel a sense of both hope and joy.

JEAN ZARU
OCCUPIED WEST BANK (RAMALLAH)

*A*t one time our good Lord said: "All things shall be well"; and at another he said: "You shall see yourself that all manner of thing shall be well." Many evil deeds are done in our sight, and such great harm taken, that it seems to us impossible that things should ever come to a good end. As we look on these, we sorrow and mourn for them, so that we cannot rest in the blissful beholding of God—as we ought to. The cause is that in the use of our reason we are now so blind, so lowly, and so simple that we cannot know the high marvelous wisdom, the power, and the goodness of the blissful Trinity. When he said, "You shall see yourself that all manner of thing shall be well," it was as if he said: "Accept it now faithfully and trustingly, and at the last end you shall see in truth and in fullness of joy."

JULIAN OF NORWICH

ENGLAND (C. 1342–AFTER 1413)

I am no longer afraid of death.
I know well
it's dark, cold corridors
leading to life.

I am afraid rather of that life
which does not come out of death,
which cramps our hands
and slows our march.

I am afraid of my fear
and even more of the fear of others,
who do not know where they are going,
who continue clinging
to what they think is life
which we know to be death!

I live each day to kill death:
I die each day to give birth to life,
and in this death of death.
I die a thousand times

and am reborn another thousand
through that love
from my People,
which nourishes hope!

JULIA ESQUIVEL

GUATEMALA (IN EXILE, UNITED STATES)

I believe, although everything
   hides you from my faith.
I believe, although everything shouts No! to me . . .
I believe, although everything may seem to die.
I believe, although I no longer would wish to live,
   because I have founded my life
   on a sincere word,
   on the word of a Friend,
   on the word of God.

I believe, although I feel alone in pain.
I believe, although I see people hating.
I believe, although I see children weep,
   because I have learnt with certainty
   that he comes to meet us
   in the hardest hours,
   with his love and his light.
I believe, but increase my faith.

BRAZILIAN HYMN

Sometimes the trials and difficulties which befall put us in the position of a traveller who suddenly finds himself on the edge of an abyss from which it is impossible to turn back. The abyss is the darkness of ignorance, and terror at being captive to death. Only the energy of a saintly despair will get us across. Upheld by some mysterious strength, we cast ourselves into the unknown, calling upon the Name of the Lord. And what happens? Instead of smashing our heads against unseen rocks, we feel an invisible hand gently carrying us over, and we come to no harm. Throwing ourselves into the unknown means trusting to God, having let go of all hope in the great ones of the earth, and setting off in search of a new life in which first place is given to Christ.

Traversing the abyss of the unknown can also be likened to swinging along a cable stretched from one side to the other. The hands of Christ crucified link the far ends of the abyss. The soul that has been given the dread privilege of travelling along this cable can find no words to describe it, just as those who have passed beyond the grave cannot tell us of their experience on the new plane.

ARCHIMANDRITE SOPHRONY
GREECE / ENGLAND (1896–1993)

*W*ith my Christ I have ever been,
With my Christ, I am now,
With my Christ, I will be forever;
In or out of suffering,
    you only will I confess.

NESTOR OF MAGYDUS
(MARTYRED 251)

CHAPTER 10

Called to Vulnerability

(Jesus Is Stripped of His Garments)

The Roman guards' act of stripping Jesus was an unambiguous assertion of their power over him. Nakedness has almost no rival as a graphic declaration of vulnerability. Is there a message for us in this picture of Jesus' absence of protection?

If God has shown willingness to suffer, to join in the anguish of human life, to become vulnerable and wounded, then, urges Desmond Tutu, believers should be surprised "not by suffering and persecution but by their absence." To live out Christ's passion is to assent to a calling that might from time to time earn the church the name church of martyrs. It might earn individual believers contempt for what appears on the surface to be their frailty and powerlessness.

But those who are weak in the eyes of beholders are inwardly driven by a strong sense of compassion and courage. Their vision penetrates pretense and flashy diversions to see the truth—to weep at misery, to speak up and pay dearly, to find prophets not in those "who wait by the ladder to heaven," according to Mother Maria Skobtsova, but in the "restless, orphaned, poor." "Stripped" Christians bear suffering because of their love and open themselves not to domination but to service.

God's plan for humanity is health, wholeness, justice. But this is a decidedly broken world, with systems and individuals at odds with God's humanizing purposes. A genuine openness to Christ, to continuing his redemptive ministry, may therefore expose us to a love that lays us open then asks that as we rise up we continue to bear our wounds.

*I*n many ways, Jesus declares, the attitude of the world and its authorities will help to determine his true followers. That treatment will be one of the criteria to help distinguish the true from the false Church (John 15:18–21). Consequently, we must not be taken aback at suffering and persecution which come our way. . . . In my view, since the cross is so central to the life and work of Jesus Christ and makes him into the sort of Saviour he is for this sort of world, the cross and suffering must be central also to the life and work of the Christian.

If this is so and Scripture seems to declare that it is so (Paul for instance declares that we can participate in the glory of the Resurrection only if we share in his suffering and death), then it must mean that surprise must be occasioned for the Christian not by suffering and persecution but by their absence. A Christian or a Church that does not suffer is a contradiction in terms. It is as meaningless and ridiculous as a Christ without the passion and death.

DESMOND TUTU
SOUTH AFRICA

*I*t is all very well to have slogans printed on our coffee mugs, "Life's a bitch, and then you die," as long as we can giggle together when we read them. But if we must begin faith by affirming life's tragic character and, in fact, find God in the tragic, such a faith will scarcely sell in America. Americans are into self-fulfillment, success, the necessity of self-esteem, and the uses of power. We admire mastery. We applaud people who have "got themselves together." In a land where denominations compete for the American soul, a religion that admits that life is inevitably tragic and "then we die" will lose out.

. . . To step from Palm Sunday immediately to Easter Day retains the note of triumph we crave. The truth is that we are embarrassed by the crucified Christ. For if Jesus on the cross is the revealing of God, then the church may be called to a very different social role, namely, to suffer and die for the world.

DAVID BUTTRICK
UNITED STATES

*A*n ordination photo of Father Ellacuria, murdered Jesuit of El Salvador, shows him vested, prostrate on the sanctuary floor while the litany of saints is chanted over the new priests. A photo dated Thursday, November 16, 1989, shows Father Ellacuria murdered, prostrate outside the Jesuit house. He is in exactly the position of his ordination rite.

The church from time to time (and wondrously in our own time) earns the name church of martyrs. It does not mean, obviously, that all the faithful perish. It signifies the living consonance between the witness of those who die and those who survive. Both speak up, both pay dearly; some in blood, some in the bearing of infamy and danger.

DANIEL BERRIGAN, S.J.
UNITED STATES

*F*or the church, abuses of human life, liberty, and dignity
are a heartfelt suffering.
The church, entrusted with the earth's glory,
believes that in each person is the creator's image
and that everyone who tramples it offends God. . . .
The church takes as spittle in its face,
   as lashes on its back,
   as the cross in its passion,
all that human beings suffer,
even though they be unbelievers. They suffer as God's images.
There is no dichotomy between man and God's image.
Whoever tortures a human being,
whoever abuses a human being, whoever outrages a human
   being,
abuses God's image, and the church takes as its own
that cross, that martyrdom.

OSCAR ROMERO
EL SALVADOR (1917−1980)

*P*erhaps Mary Magdalene, weeping over Jesus' murder, is the clearest witness to the pain that characterizes the Christian minority's feeling about life in this world of persecution and the triumph of injustice. Mary Magdalene neither accuses God nor defends God; she weeps, which means she is far deeper in God than accusation or defense can be. To accuse—or to defend—she would have to have a distance from God; she would have run away like the male disciples. But she is *in* God's pain and surrounded by it. "Truly, truly I say to you," says the Johannine Christ, "you will weep and lament, but the world will rejoice" (John 16:20). The ones who rejoice are those who cheer the triumphal marches of the Roman Caesars when yet another conquered people is forced to its knees, pillaged, raped, and sold into slavery. The world will rejoice—these are the glittering gladiatorial combats and sports shows the Romans hold to distract persons from the misery of hunger. "You will weep and lament," because, in a world of legalized violence, each word that speaks seriously of justice and peace is clubbed down and mocked. The Romans knew exactly what a threat the Christian community posed to the politico-religious state consensus.

DOROTHEE SÖLLE

GERMANY

*T*here are no prophecies. Only life
continuously acts as prophet.
The end approaches, days grow shorter.
You took a servant's form. Hosanna.

I searched for singers and for prophets
who wait by the ladder to heaven,
see signs of the mysterious end,
sing songs beyond our comprehension.

And I found people who were restless, orphaned, poor,
drunk, despairing, useless,
lost whichever way they went,
homeless, naked, lacking bread.

MOTHER MARIA SKOBTSOVA
ROMANIA (1891–1945)

On Calvary, on the altar, Christ makes himself not invulnerable but vulnerable. He lays himself bare to the hand of friend and enemy alike. On the cross he was one great wound from head to foot, the nerves that should be hidden were exposed, the body was rent and open; the tenderest touch of his mother's hand would have inflicted the keenest agony, for those nerves and muscles which should be covered lay exposed and bare. As so it must always be in proportion as we love. It is an inevitable result of love upon his earth that, in loving, we give to the beloved the power of paining us; and the greater our love the greater also the corresponding power. For to love is, as it were, to lay heart and soul open to our friend; it is to strip ourselves, not only of all artificial armour, but even of the covering that Nature herself provides for the feelings and the heart. And this is the love that Christ has for all men: the best and the worst have power to wound because he gives it to them by the mere fact of his love.

MAUDE PETRE
ENGLAND (1863–1942)

I shall struggle to live the reality of Christ's rising and death's dying. In my living, my son's dying will not be the last word. But as I rise up, I bear the wounds of his death. My rising does not remove them. They mark me. If you want to know who I am, put your hand in.

NICHOLAS WOLTERSTORFF
UNITED STATES

Outwardly Christians stumble and fall from time to time. Only weakness and shame appear on the surface, revealing that the Christians are sinners who do that which displeases the world. Then they are regarded as fools, Cinderellas, as footmats for the world, as damned, impotent, and worthless people. But this does not matter. In their weakness, sin, folly, and frailty there abides inwardly and secretly a force and power unrecognizable by the world and hidden from its view, but one which, for all that, carries off the victory, for Christ resides in them and manifests Himself to them. I have seen many of these who, externally, tottered along very feebly, but when it came to the test and they faced the court, Christ bestirred Himself in them, and they became so staunch that the devil had to flee.

MARTIN LUTHER
GERMANY (1483–1546)

CHAPTER 11

Identifying with the Pain of Jesus
(Jesus Is Nailed to the Cross)

Our forebears were unable to hide from pain and death; they had no hospitals in which to isolate the dying. Today it is all too easy for us in technologically saturated, fenced-in society to separate ourselves from the pain of others. Sometimes pain becomes so foreign that it makes us uncomfortable and disconcerted.

The pain of Jesus on the cross can have the same effect. Sometimes we distance ourselves by looking at Jesus' death only as it has been rendered picturesque and historical—a stained-glass-window approach. But the death of Jesus, according to Dorothy L. Sayers, was "a bloody, dusty, sweaty, and sordid business," a fully human death, which should shock us.

Another way that we may insulate ourselves from Jesus' pain and death is by claiming that in his divinity Jesus didn't feel all that we do. But

Jesus' pain was not less; it was more. "Alive to all that is lovely and true, lawful and right," as George MacDonald puts it, Jesus more deeply experienced the "breach of the harmony of things whose sound is torture." Jesus' death was also more because, according to Denise Levertov, "He took to Himself the sum total of anguish and drank even the lees of that cup" as "every sorrow and desolation he saw, and sorrowed in kinship."

To focus on Jesus' painful death may seem to be morbid or to smack of shame-based religion. In a sunny suburb with the mall a mile away, we can discuss the cross as negative, the pain of Jesus as a bit extreme. But we find sincerity and integrity in those whose faith has been hammered out in the crucible of extreme pressure. From a South African jail, a fourteenth-century plague, or a desperately poor ghetto, voices encourage us to re-examine the pain of Jesus. His pain becomes close and tangible, and we find that we no longer want to distance ourselves from it.

*G*od was executed by people painfully like us, in a society very similar to our own—in the over-ripeness of the most splendid and sophisticated Empire the world has ever seen. In a nation famous for its religious genius and under a government renowned for its efficiency, He was executed by a corrupt church, a timid politician, and a fickle proletariat led by professional agitators. His executioners made vulgar jokes about Him, called Him filthy names, taunted Him, smacked Him in the face, flogged Him with the cat, and hanged Him on the common gibbet—a bloody, dusty, sweaty, and sordid business.

If you show people that, they are shocked. So they should be. If that does not shock them, nothing can. If the mere representation of it has an air of irreverence, what is to be said about the deed? It is curious that people who are filled with horrified indignation whenever a cat kills a sparrow can hear that story of the killing of God told Sunday after Sunday and not experience any shock at all.

DOROTHY L. SAYERS
ENGLAND (1893–1957)

*I*t is with the holiest fear that we should approach the terrible fact of the sufferings of Our Lord. Let no one think that these were less because He was more. The more delicate the nature, the more alive to all that is lovely and true, lawful and right, the more does it feel the antagonism of pain, the inroad of death upon life; the more dreadful is that breach of the harmony of things whose sound is torture.

GEORGE MACDONALD
SCOTLAND (1824–1905)

*E*very sorrow and desolation He saw, and sorrowed in kinship.

JULIAN OF NORWICH
ENGLAND (C. 1342–AFTER 1413)

On a Theme from Julian's Chapter XX

Six hours outstretched in the sun, yes,
hot wood, the nails, blood trickling
into the eyes, yes—
but the thieves on their neighbor crosses
survived till after the soldiers
had come to fracture their legs, or longer.
Why single out this agony? What's
a mere six hours?
Torture then, torture now,
the same, the pain's the same,
immemorial branding iron,

electric prod.
Hasn't a child
dazed in the hospital ward they reserve
for the most abused, known worse?
This air we're breathing,
these very clouds, ephemeral billows
languid upon the sky's
moody ocean, we share
with women and men who've held out
days and weeks on the rack—
and in the ancient dust of the world what particles
of the long tormented,
what ashes.

But Julian's lucid spirit leapt
to the difference:
perceived why no awe could measure
that brief day's endless length,
why among all the tortured
One only is "King of Grief."
The oneing, she saw, *the oneing
with the Godhead* opened Him utterly
to the pain of all minds, all bodies

—sands of the sea, of the desert—
from first beginning
to last day. The great wonder is
that the human cells of His flesh and bone
didn't explode
when utmost Imagination rose
in that flood of knowledge. Unique
in agony, Infinite strength, Incarnate,
empowered Him to endure
inside of history,
through those hours when He took to Himself
the sum total of anguish and drank
even the lees of that cup:

within the mesh of the web, Himself
woven within it, yet seeing it,
seeing it whole. *Every sorrow and desolation
He saw, and sorrowed in kinship.*

DENISE LEVERTOV
UNITED STATES (1923–1997)

*L*ove makes the whole difference between an execution and a martyrdom. Pain, and the willingness to risk pain, alone gives dignity and worth to human love and is the price of its creative power; without that, it is mere emotional enjoyment. It costs a lot to love any human being, even our nearest and dearest, to the bitter end. So God loved the world. And so too love and pain, tension, effort, loneliness, endurance, self-giving: these rule and condition all the victories of art and science and adventure. The Cross is the price of all real achievement.

EVELYN UNDERHILL
ENGLAND (1875–1941)

*N*ails could not have held God-made-Man fastened to a tree,
had not love held him there.

CATHERINE OF SIENA

(1347–1380)

*T*ell us further, you African: what of Jesus, the Christ,
Born in Bethlehem: Son of Man and Son of God
Do you believe in him?"
The answer is:
"For ages he eluded us, this Jesus of Bethlehem, Son of
   Man:
Going first to Asia and to Europe, and the western
   sphere . . .
Later on, he came, this Son of Man:
Like a child delayed he came to us.

The white man brought him.
He was pale, and not the sunburnt son of the desert.
As a child he came.

A wee little babe wrapped in swaddling clothes.
Ah, if only he had been little Moses, lying
Sun-scorched on the banks of the River of God
We would have recognized him.
He eludes us still, this Jesus, Son of Man.
His words: Ah, they taste so good
As sweet and refreshing as the sap of the palm
raised and nourished on African soil.
The Truths of his words are for all men, for all time.

And yet for us it is when he is on the cross,
This Jesus of Nazareth, with holed hands
and open side, like a beast at a sacrifice;
When he is stripped naked like us,
Browned and sweating water and blood in the heat
of the sun,
Yet silent,
That we cannot resist him.

How like us he is, this Jesus of Nazareth,
Beaten, tortured, imprisoned, spat upon, truncheoned,
Denied by his own, and chased like a thief in the night,
Despised, and rejected like a dog that has fleas,
for NO REASON."

GABRIEL SETILOANE
SOUTH AFRICA

*J*esus cries out, "I am thirsty," expressing the agony of the one who suffers. This cry rises out of the depths of Jesus' being, "I suffer; I am in need." It is the primal scream of all suffering. . . .

This cry echoes through the ages in the voices of all who thirst and hunger, or who ache for companionship, freedom, or justice. It is the scream of suffering in our world, echoing Jesus' agony on the cross.

If we are faithful, we must respond to this cry and alleviate misery. The strategy for this is a political and economic one, open to analysis and discussion. But the misery itself is not for analysis. It is to be heard, absorbed, and recognized as holy ground.

LORETTA GIRZAITIS AND RICHARD L. WOOD

UNITED STATES

*P*erhaps there is a mother here whose son is a prisoner in Russia. Every day she experiences afresh in her heart the lostness, the homesickness and the comfortless slave routine of her child. Indeed, this fellow-suffering of the mother's heart is perhaps more painful and tormenting than that suffered by the distant son. This is just a feeble reflection of what the Saviour goes through on the hill of Golgotha. His infinite understanding leads Him to suffer vicariously all that separates men from His Father. The dicers, the harlots, the executioners, the tax-gatherers, the Pharisees—they do not know how lost and far from home they are. They forget it in play or gambling or dreaming. But the Son of God knows the desperate need of all of them. His love gives Him such sharp vision. He knows, and He bears it all with them and for them.

HELMUT THIELICKE
GERMANY (1908–1985)

CHAPTER 12

Understanding the Cross

(Jesus Dies on the Cross)

*W*hy did it happen? What was accomplished on the cross? How do we respond? Christians have spent centuries attempting to fathom the meaning of Christ's death and its implications for our lives.

In this chapter we listen as Christians from the 300s to the 1990s offer answers to the *whys* and *therefores* of the cross and Jesus' death.

That Jesus' extraordinary ministry was terminated so abruptly and prematurely should perhaps not surprise us. His message, the Gospels clearly show, was not entirely popular with those in power. He represented an "intolerable threat," in Walter Wink's words, to a system based on domination and supremacy. Living out his liberating message with unswerving commitment, Jesus would not compromise his convictions in order to save his life. The way Jesus lived, therefore, brought about the way he died. A displeased deity demanding payment for sin did not kill Jesus. Human beings—threatened and cowardly, under the sway of Powers at cross-purposes with God's intent for human wholeness—caused Jesus' death.

The "Good" in Good Friday is that the cross, a tragedy transformed by God, has come to embody the power of healing, reconciliation, and hope. The man who was Life endured ignominious death: This wonder has inspired his followers and evoked gratitude. He has affirmed our own struggles and integrity and has offered us "saving companionship," as Kallistos Ware says in this chapter. His courageous acceptance of the cross has put to flight all our mistaken notions of passive self-sacrifice and victimization. In Jesus' death on the cross we hear a strange silence that in fact shouts the love and solidarity that characterized Jesus' mission.

O holy Wisdom of our God,
eternally offensive to our wisdom,
and compassionate towards our weakness,
we praise you and give you thanks,
because you emptied yourself of power
and entered our struggle,
taking upon you our unprotected flesh.
You opened wide your arms for us upon the cross,
becoming scandal for our sake,
that you might sanctify even the grave
to be a bed of hope to your people.

Therefore, with those who are detained without justice,
abandoned or betrayed by friends,
whose bodies are violated or in pain;
with those who have died alone
without dignity, comfort, or hope;
and with all the company of saints
who have carried you in their wounds

that they may be bodied forth with life,
we praise you, saying:

Holy, holy, holy,
vulnerable God.
Heaven and earth are full of your glory;
hosanna in the highest.
Blessed is the one
who comes in the name of God;
hosanna in the highest.

JANET MORLEY
ENGLAND

*G*od surely anticipated that a person like Jesus would be killed by an order established on violence, but God did not kill Jesus, or require his death, or manipulate others into sacrificing him. God may have found a way to triumph over this crime, but God did not cause it. Jesus was killed by the definite plan and malice aforethought of the Powers, as the New Testament writers clearly state.

They had to kill him, for Jesus represented the most intolerable threat ever placed against the spirituality, values, and arrangements of the Domination System. . . .

Not only did he and his followers repudiate the androcratic values of power and wealth, but the institutions and systems that authorized and supported these values: the family, the Law, the sacrificial system, the Temple, kosher food regulations, the distinction between clean and unclean, patriarchy, role expectations for women and children, the class system, the use of violence, racial and ethnic divisions, the distinction between insider and outsider—indeed, every conceivable prop of domination, division, and supremacy.

WALTER WINK
UNITED STATES

139

Nailed to a cross because you would not
compromise on your convictions.
Nailed to a cross because you would not
bow down before insolent might.
My Saviour, you were laughed at,
derided, bullied, and spat upon
but with unbroken spirit,
Liberator God, you died.

Many young lives are sacrificed
because they will not bend;
many young people in prison
for following your lead.
Daily, you are crucified
my Saviour, you are sacrificed
in prison cells and torture rooms
of cruel and ruthless powers.

The promise of resurrection,
the power of hope it holds,
and the vision of a just new order
you proclaimed that first Easter morning.

Therefore, dear Saviour, we can affirm
that although bodies are mutilated and broken,
the spirit refuses submission.
Your voice will never be silenced,
Great Liberating God.

ARUNA GNANADASON

INDIA

*T*he cross ... discloses the depth of human sin. It is a triumph of demonolatry and a defeat of a God domesticated by an organized religion. But of course a domesticated God is not the true God. The cross reveals the impotence *not* of the God of Jesus but the God of those who conspired to put Jesus to death, the God who had to acquiesce in the evil plans hatched in the inmost part of the religion that held that God captive. The cross, in short, is human violence and not divine violence.

CHOAN∗SENG SONG

SOUTH KOREA

*F*or women, the sacrificial love of Jesus on the cross requires reinterpretation in which Jesus' act is clearly seen as a free and active choice in the face of an evil that has been resisted. It is not passive victimization. Nor did God require a sacrificial death. Jesus died because of the way he lived, because of the pattern of fidelity and commitment of his life and his liberating message. The ideal of self-sacrificial love is the ultimate Christ model, to be followed at extreme moments in human history, in martyrdom. "Imitation" of Jesus, discipleship, following, in relation to the Gospel witness of his message, ministry, and way of life, no longer connote passive self-sacrifice but an active, indeed even a subversive freedom in relation to God and to religious and societal structures.

ANNE E. CARR
UNITED STATES

*T*he Lord crucified Himself for the world before the world crucified Him. He carried out the offering of His body, His self, as a sacrifice on behalf of the world immediately after He was baptized when He was led by the Spirit.

. . . It would appear that the crucifixion was the final act of the Lord, but it was in fact the theme of His entire life.

MATTHEW THE POOR OF EGYPT

*T*he cross is the way of the lost
the cross is the staff of the lame
the cross is the guide of the blind
the cross is the strength of the weak
the cross is the hope of the hopeless
the cross is the freedom of the slaves
the cross is the water of the seeds
the cross is the consolation of the bonded labourers
the cross is the source of those who seek water
the cross is the cloth of the naked.

FROM A TENTH·CENTURY
AFRICAN HYMN

*I*magine Christ our Lord present before you upon the cross, and begin to speak with him, asking how it is that though He is the Creator, He has stooped to become man, and to pass from eternal life to death here in time, that thus He might die for our sins.

I shall also reflect upon myself and ask:

"What have I done for Christ?"

"What am I doing for Christ?"

"What ought I to do for Christ?"

As I behold Christ in this plight, nailed to the cross, I shall ponder upon what presents itself to my mind.

IGNATIUS OF LOYOLA

(1491–1556)

*W*e should not say that Christ has suffered "instead of us," but rather that he has suffered *on our behalf.* The Son of God suffered "unto death," not that we might be exempt from suffering, but that our suffering might be like his. Christ offers us, not a way *round* suffering, but a way *through* it; not substitution, but saving companionship.

KALLISTOS WARE
ENGLAND

*F*or it is only on the cross that a man dies with his hands spread out.

ATHANASIUS
EGYPT (C. 296–373)

*T*he cross is the most universal symbol of Christianity. But often we forget that the symbol of our salvation was originally a tree growing somewhere, probably among many other trees. Those who cut it down had not the slightest idea that it would one day become the most universal symbol of millions upon millions of Christians. They thought nothing about the fact that on that tree God would be crucified in order to reconcile the world to himself; that on that tree redemption was to flow from God to mankind in a once-and-for-all act of self-sacrifice. . . .

This is the tree which causes discomfort to the world, which has turned the world upside-down. It is the tree which the world cannot erase, cannot get rid of, and cannot forget. The tree of the cross has built bridges across rivers and valleys; it has brought people of different backgrounds together; it has torn down barriers and pierced through walls of separation; it has crossed oceans and travelled afar to tell people the good news which it heard one Friday morning two thousand years ago. Indeed this tree has been persecuted, whacked with axes, shot at with bullets, hanged, beaten, given to wild beasts, torn to pieces, chopped up, ostracized, burned, laughed at, condemned, and made to suffer many other things. This tree bears upon itself thousands of scars and wounds. Yet in spite of them all, it has continued to heal the sick, to bring hope to the desperate, to comfort the oppressed, to guide the lost, to feed the hungry, to shelter the poor, to inspire the anxious, to illumine the intellectual, to challenge the fearless, to save the condemned and to meet the needs of every generation and every human situation. What a tree!

JOHN MBITI

KENYA

So Christ in us forgives all that is past and strengthens us to find that amendment of life, that real Christian maturity we seek. As we turn more and more to the Christ within us, his personality permeates ours, his radiance gradually burns through the protective devices we have set up against him and other people, and one day we are free, redeemed, saved by the cross of Christ.

This is one way of sketching the saving power of the cross of Christ. The Church has never defined the doctrine of the Atonement, has never sought to be exact and precise in its accounts of the redemption won by Christ. Instead, it goes on celebrating it in hymn and liturgy, and Christians go on experiencing it in their lives. However, there are certain key elements in it to which we must hold: our salvation is won by an act of sacrificial self-offering by Jesus that shocks us into a true awareness of our own condition. This is followed by the healing experience of forgiveness, and the knowledge that Jesus is within us, changing us into his own likeness. . . . Christ hangs there before us, beseeching us to stay and look, and as we gaze upon him, the awful picture of sin's curse becomes at the very same time a shining image of the unconquerable love and mercy of God. This is how the redeeming work is still done today, if only we will stay long enough to see what is really going on.

RICHARD HOLLOWAY

SCOTLAND

*K*illing Jesus was like trying to destroy a dandelion seed-head by blowing on it. It was like shattering a sun into a million fragments of light.

WALTER WINK

UNITED STATES

151

CHAPTER 13

The Near Presence

(The Body of Jesus Is Placed in the Arms of His Mother)

*A*rtists have been particularly drawn to depicting that moment when Mary held Jesus' lifeless body. These pietas usually portray a tender closeness and intimacy. This visual image speaks to a reality that Christians experience: the nearness of the living Christ. In his life on earth and beyond, Christ was not and is not elevated and remote. The writers in this chapter remind us that Jesus did not stay on the cross, but that he has been brought down and revealed to us.

Christ has come down from the cross into our situations—plunging into the world's passions, anticipations, sufferings. In so doing he has taken on our human condition and has freely chosen to be present not only with us, but in us. At this stopping place, we are asked to let ourselves be comforted with assurances that we cannot be separated from Jesus. When we cry out in our aloneness, we find we are not alone. We find ourselves, as Martin Marty says in this chapter, "in company, in his company." Even in cruel losses, Jesus' presence keeps us. These writers affirm that there is no cry unheard and that there is one with us, who shares the darkness.

*C*hrist is alive! No longer bound to distant years in Palestine,
    but saving, healing, here and now, and touching every place
      and time.
    In every insult, rift and war, where color, scorn or wealth
      divide,
    Christ suffers still, yet loves the more, and lives, where even
      hope has died.

BRIAN A. WREN
ENGLAND

*I*t is not true that "God tries those whom he loves." But it is true
    that the more we suffer, the more Christ is present in us.

MICHEL QUOIST
FRANCE

154

*W*e cannot shed a tear, but that tear has already blinded the eyes of Christ. We cannot be without tears, but that constriction of the heart has constricted His Heart. He has known all and every kind of fear that we know, and there is no possible loneliness, no agony of separation, but it is Christ's; indeed, not one of us can die, but it is Christ dying. And Christ, Who faces all these things in our lives, has overcome them all and has sanctified them by His limitless love. His love made every moment of His Passion redeeming and healing and life-giving, and this love, this Christ-love, is ours, just as much as His suffering is.

CARYLL HOUSELANDER
ENGLAND (1901–1954)

O Risen Christ, you go down
to the lowest depths of our human condition,
and you burden yourself
with what burdens us. . . .

And even when within us
we can hear no refrain
of your presence,
you are there.
Through your Holy Spirit
you remain within us.

BROTHER ROGER
OF TAIZE

The only serious mistake we can make when illness comes, when anxiety threatens, when conflict disturbs our relationships with others is to conclude that God has gotten bored in looking after us and has shifted his attention to a more exciting Christian, or that God has become disgusted with our meandering obedience and decided to let us fend for ourselves for a while, or that God has gotten too busy fulfilling prophecy in the Middle East to take time now to sort out the complicated mess we have gotten ourselves into. That is the *only* serious mistake we can make. It is the mistake that Psalm 121 prevents: the mistake of supposing that God's interest in us waxes and wanes in response to our spiritual temperature.

EUGENE H. PETERSON
UNITED STATES

*D*o not look forward to what might happen tomorrow; the same everlasting Father who cares for you today, will take care of you tomorrow and every day. Either He will shield you from suffering or He will give you unfailing strength to bear it. Be at peace, then, and put aside all anxious thoughts and imaginings.

FRANCIS DE SALES
SWITZERLAND (1567–1622)

*P*hysical pain was not the point [of Jesus' cry from the cross]. Spiritual abandonment was. . . . In this plot, the point is precisely that Jesus does experience abandonment. *"My God, my God, why hast thou forsaken me?"*

When I am henceforth lost in the wintry night, alone, I identify exactly with a cry already uttered: "O my god, I cry in the daytime but thou dost not answer, in the night I cry but get no respite" (Psalm 22:2). The world in front of this text opens to me the possibility that by uttering the prayer, a prayer of aloneness, I am not only alone. Someone in whom I trust has shouted it out before, in worse circumstances. What is more, Jesus cried out because a pledge seemed to be broken, and that seemingly was turning to reality. *Because* it seemed so, it *was* being broken. He was not supposed to be abandoned, yet he was abandoned.

. . . The crucified victim was the *only* forsaken one, the true derelict. The rest of us die in company, in *his* company. God certified his gift and his act and "raised him up." Never again is aloneness to be so stark for others.

MARTIN MARTY
UNITED STATES

I have called to God and heard no answer,
I have seen the thick curtain drop and sunlight die;
My voice has echoed back, a foolish voice,
The prayer restored intact
to its silly source.
I have walked in darkness, he hung in it.
In all my mines of night, he was there first;
In whatever dead tunnel I am lost, he finds me.
My God, my God, why has thou forsaken me?
From his perfect darkness a voice says, "I have not."

CHAD WALSH

UNITED STATES (1914–1991)

I believe,
no pain is lost.
No tear unmarked,
no cry of anguish
dies unheard,
lost in the hail of gunfire
or blanked out by the padded cell.
I believe that pain
and prayer
are somehow saved,
processed,
stored,
used in the Divine Economy.
The blood shed in Salvador
will irrigate the heart
of some financier
a million miles away.
The terror,
pain,
despair,
swamped
by lava, flood or earthquake

will be caught up
like mist and fall again,
a gentle rain
on arid hearts
or souls despairing
in the back streets
of Brooklyn.

SHEILA CASSIDY
ENGLAND

*C*hrist be with me, Christ within me,
Christ behind me, Christ before me,
Christ beside me, Christ to win me,
Christ to comfort and restore me,
Christ beneath me, Christ above me,
Christ in quiet, Christ in danger,
Christ in hearts of all that love me,
Christ in mouth of friend and stranger.

ATTRIBUTED TO ST. PATRICK
IRELAND (C. 390–460)

CHAPTER 14

Life Answers Death

(Jesus Is Laid in the Tomb)

*W*hen Jesus was laid in the tomb, it seemed to his followers that the
light of their lives had been extinguished. Luke tells us that some of the
women, including Mary Magdalene, went from Golgotha to see where
Jesus' body was laid. As the women kissed their beloved teacher before the
tomb was closed, they must have felt the last warmth leaving his body.
Jesus was dead, and with him the dream of a new way of living.

We know what they could not, that God "shakes heaven and earth," to
use Janet Morley's words: Jesus rose from the dead. So although the four-
teenth station of the cross is traditionally associated with Jesus being laid
in the tomb, most writers and dramatists cannot contain their resurrection joy. From this side of the resurrection, they see the paradox that is
central to our Christian faith: What appears to have the upper hand—
pain, cruelty, death—is overcome by life and joy.

Although Jesus was laid in the tomb, the tomb could not contain him. This was great news not only for Jesus' first disciples, but for all his later followers who face darkness, suffering, and death. Not content to raise only Jairus's daughter or Lazarus, Jesus entered into death and grappled with that twistedness at the heart of human experience and "has destroyed death by undergoing death," in the words of an ancient Easter hymn. The writers in this chapter remind us that Christ has trampled fear and darkness.

They invite us to join them in their resurrection joy.

The resurrection—first revealed to those who were weak in society—creates a new community, as voices from a Soviet concentration camp or an oppressed African-American community testify. But they not only invite us to celebrate in the "already" of Christ's resurrection, they also challenge us to press forward, sowing "the seeds of justice and freedom" and breaking "the chains of humiliation and death." We can do this because we know that even the threat of death is in fact a threat of resurrection. Indeed, as Marjorie Hewott Suchocki declares, "Resurrection answers crucifixion; life answers death."

*T*he edges of God are tragedy; the depths of God are joy, beauty, resurrection, life. Resurrection answers crucifixion; life answers death.

MARJORIE HEWITT SUCHOCKI
UNITED STATES

*R*ejoice, heavenly powers! Sing, choirs of angels!
Exult, all creation around God's throne!
Jesus Christ, our King, is risen!
Sound the trumpet of salvation!

Rejoice, O earth, in shining splendour,
radiant in the brightness of your King!
Christ has conquered! Glory fills you!
Darkness vanishes for ever!

Rejoice, O Mother Church! Exult in glory!
The risen Savior shines upon you!
Let this place resound with joy,
echoing the mighty song of all God's people!

EASTER VIGIL LITURGY

On Easter Day all of us who were imprisoned for religious convictions were united in the one joy of Christ. We were all taken into one feeling, into one spiritual triumph, glorifying the one eternal God. There was no solemn Paschal service with the ringing of church bells, no possibility in our camp to gather for worship, to dress up for the festival, to prepare Easter dishes. On the contrary, there was even more work and more interference than usual. All the prisoners here for religious convictions, whatever their denomination, were surrounded by more spying, by more threats from the secret police.

Yet Easter was there: great, holy, spiritual, unforgettable. It was blessed by the presence of our risen God among us—blessed by the silent Siberian stars and by our sorrows. How our hearts beat joyfully in communion with the great Resurrection! Death is conquered, fear no more, an eternal Easter is given to us! Full of this marvellous Easter, we send you from our prison camp the victorious and joyful tidings: Christ is risen!

LETTER FROM A
SOVIET CONCENTRATION CAMP

*B*lack Christians have been especially aware that to be Christian is to be "Easter People.". . . How many times when the way gets dark and dreary, the road rough and rocky, the problems great and discouraging, the black preacher has reminded a beleaguered and discouraged flock: "It's Friday now, but Sunday's coming!" Christians do not remain at the cross where crucifixion and death hold sway. Part of the great contribution of the black worship and preaching tradition has been not only to face realistically the burdens and troubles of this world, but to find the grace notes in a sad song, to affirm hope in the midst of debilitating despair, to find a "bright side somewhere." That bright side for black Christians, and all who will believe, is on the other side of the empty tomb, beyond Friday—because Sunday does come!

WILLIAM B. MCCLAIN
UNITED STATES

Now the green blade riseth from the buried grain,
wheat that in dark earth many days has lain;
love lives again, that with the dead has been:
Love is come again like wheat that springeth green.

In the grave they laid him, Love whom hate had slain,
thinking that never he would wake again,
laid in the earth like grain that sleeps unseen:
Love is come again like wheat that springeth green.

Forth he came at Easter, like the risen grain,
he that for three days in the grave had lain,
quick from the dead my risen Lord is seen:
Love is come again like wheat that springeth green.

When our hearts are wintry, grieving, or in pain,
thy touch can call us back to life again,
fields of our hearts that dead and bare have been:
Love is come again like wheat that springeth green.

JOHN MACLEOD CAMPBELL CRUM
SCOTLAND (1872–1958)

*T*he Resurrection becomes a tangible fact in a very different way from that which we should expect. Not by direct empirical verification but by the radical transformation of the community into a fellowship of justice, truth, compassion, reconciliation and sharing of all things, is the presence and power of the risen Jesus known.

MONIKA K. HELLWIG

UNITED STATES

*T*he women in the life of Jesus were there—caring, loving, suffering. Is this God's way of moving from the center to the periphery of life, of reversing the masculine logic of supremacy to show that the authentic bearers of God's truth are those on the periphery who in their weakness know of no source of power except that which comes from the Lord? . . .

Women in our own time still find themselves on the periphery of life. We should, must and ought to resent it, but we must also transform that resentment to care for and struggle with those similarly victimized by racism, sexism and other forms of discrimination. It is by that road that Easter becomes reality. Jesus brought Easter about that way. The women of the New Testament discovered Easter that way. It should not be any different for us.

For they who were in the background, serving, caring and suffering, were allowed to be the first witnesses to the risen Lord! The first to see the resurrected Christ! The first to tell of the good news! And though fearful, they were also filled with tremendous joy.

The same good news is given to our broken world. The Lord comes unexpectedly, in mysterious ways, to the weak, the poor, the oppressed and those placed on the periphery of this world. They will become central in his kingdom.

The same Lord comes to bring joy, strength and hope, and ultimately, life to the victims of injustice in this world.

AMELIA L. ORACIÓN

PHILIPPINES

*E*aster is, for us, not just one of the feasts, but "the Feast of Feasts and the solemn Celebration of all Celebrations." . . . Easter . . . is directed . . . to the age to come. Easter is the forecourt on earth of the manifestation of glory . . . , the forecourt of the heavenly Jerusalem which at the end of time will come down from heaven to earth. . . .

The life of the age to come is not a simple negation of this age, not its annihilation, but the making eternal of everything in it worthy of such a transformation, just as eternity is not the forgetting or abolition of time, but the establishing of its unchanging course.

SERGEI NIKOLAEVICH BULGAKOV
RUSSIA / UNITED STATES (1871–1944)

*L*et none lament his poverty; for the universal Kingdom is revealed. Let none bewail his transgressions; for the light of forgiveness has risen from the tomb. Let none fear death; for the death of the Saviour has set us free.

He has destroyed death by undergoing death.

He has despoiled hell by descending into hell.

Hell was filled with bitterness when it met thee face to face below:

filled with bitterness, for it was brought to nothing; filled with bitterness, for it was mocked;

filled with bitterness, for it was overthrown;

filled with bitterness, for it was put in chains.

It received a body, and encountered God. It received earth, and confronted heaven.

O death, where is thy sting? O hell, where is thy victory?

Christ is risen, and thou art cast down.

Christ is risen, and the demons are fallen.

ATTRIBUTED TO JOHN CHRYSOSTOM
SYRIA (C. 347–407)

When the day comes on which our victory
    will shine like a torch in the night,
    it will be like a dream.
We will laugh and sing for joy.
Then the other nations will say about us,
    "The Lord did great things for them."
Indeed, he is doing great things for us;
that is why we are happy in our suffering.

Lord, break the chains of humiliation and death,
    just as on that glorious morning
    when you were raised.
Let those who weep as they sow the seeds of justice and
    freedom,
gather the harvest of peace and reconciliation.

Those who weep as they go out as instruments of your love
    will come back singing with joy,
    as they will witness the disappearance of hate
and the manifestation of your love in your world.

ZEPHANIA KAMEETA

NAMIBIA

They Have Threatened Us with Resurrection

It isn't the noise in the streets
that keeps us from resting, my friend,
nor is it the shouts of the young people
coming out drunk from the "St. Pauli,"
nor is it the tumult of those who pass by excitedly
on their way to the mountains.

It is something within us that doesn't let us sleep,
that doesn't let us rest,
that won't stop pounding
deep inside,
it is the silent, warm weeping
of Indian women without their husbands,
it is the sad gaze of the children
fixed somewhere beyond memory,
precious in our eyes
which during sleep,
though closed, keep watch,
systole,
diastole,
awake.

Now six have left us,
and nine in Rabinál,
and two, plus two, plus two,
and ten, a hundred, a thousand,
a whole army
witness to our pain,
our fear,
our courage,
our *hope!*

What keeps us from sleeping
is that they have threatened us with Resurrection!
Because every evening
though weary of killings,
an endless inventory since 1954,
yet we go on loving life
and do not accept their death!

They have threatened us with Resurrection
because we have felt their inert bodies,
and their souls penetrated ours

doubly fortified,
because in this marathon of Hope,
there are always others to relieve us
who carry the strength
to reach the finish line
which lies beyond death.

They have threatened us with Resurrection
because they will not be able to take away from us
their bodies,
their souls,
their strength,
their spirit,
nor even their death
and least of all their life.
Because they live
today, tomorrow, and always
in the streets baptized with their blood,
in the air that absorbed their cry,
in the jungle that hid their shadows,
in the river that gathered up their laughter,
in the ocean that holds their secrets,
in the craters of the volcanoes,

Pyramids of the New Day,
which swallowed up their ashes.

They have threatened us with Resurrection,
because they are more alive than ever before,
because they transform our agonies
and fertilize our struggle,
because they pick us up when we fall,
because they loom like giants
before the crazed gorillas' fear.

They have threatened us with Resurrection,
because they do not know life (poor things!).

That is the whirlwind
which does not let us sleep,
the reason why sleeping, we keep watch,
and awake, we dream.

No, it's not the street noises,
nor the shouts from the drunks in the "St. Pauli,"
nor the noise from the fans at the ball park.
It is the internal cyclone of a kaleidoscopic struggle
which will heal that wound of the quetzal

fallen in Ixcán,
it is the earthquake soon to come
that will shake the world
and put everything in its place.

No, brother,
it is not the noise in the streets
which does not let us sleep.

Join us in this vigil
and you will know what it is to dream!
Then you will know how marvelous it is
to live threatened with Resurrection!

To dream awake,
to keep watch asleep,
to live while dying,
and to know ourselves already
resurrected!

JULIA ESQUIVEL
GUATEMALA (IN EXILE, UNITED STATES)

May the God who shakes heaven and earth,
whom death could not contain,
who lives to disturb and heal us,
bless you with power to go forth
and proclaim the gospel,
Amen.

JANET MORLEY

ENGLAND

Credits

Grateful acknowledgment is made to the following sources for their contributions to this collection. Any omissions are unintentional and will be corrected upon future printings.

CHAPTER 1

The Cost of Discipleship by Dietrich Bonhoeffer. Copyright © 1959 SCM Press, Ltd. Reprinted by permission of Macmillan Publishing Company.

To Dance with God by Gertrud Mueller Nelson. Copyright © 1986 Gertrud Mueller Nelson. Reprinted by permission of Paulist Press.

Great Lent by Alexander Schmemann. Copyright © 1969 St. Vladimir's Seminary Press. Reprinted by permission.

A Common Prayer by Michael Leunig. Copyright © 1990 Collins Dove. Reprinted by permission of the author.

Journey into Christ by Alan Jones. Copyright © 1977 Seabury Press. Reprinted by permission of the author.

The Hungering Dark by Frederick Buechner. Copyright © 1969 Frederick Buechner. Reprinted by permission of HarperCollins Publishers, Inc.

The Road Less Traveled: A New Psychology of Love, Traditional Values, and Spiritual Growth by M. Scott Peck. Copyright © 1978 M. Scott Peck, M.D. Reprinted by permission of Simon & Schuster, Inc.

Raissa's Journal: Presented by Jacques Maritain by Raissa Maritain. Copyright © 1974 Magi Books. Reprinted by permission.

Celebrating Women, eds. Janet Morley and Hannah Ward. Copyright © 1986 Janet Morley. Reprinted by permission.

CHAPTER 2

Christology at the Crossroads by Joe Sobrino. Copyright © 1978 Orbis Books. Reprinted by permission.

CHAPTER 4

The Fire of Your Life by Maggie Ross. Copyright © 1992 Maggie Ross. Reprinted by permission of HarperCollins Publishers, Inc.

How Can It Be All Right When Everything Is All Wrong? by Lewis B. Smedes. Copyright © 1982 Lewis B. Smedes. Reprinted by permission of HarperCollins Publishers, Inc.

"Only My Death Can Express My Life," by Gustávo Gutiérrez in *Way of the Cross: The Passion of Christ in the Americas,* ed. Virgil Elizondo. Copyright © 1992 Orbis Books. Reprinted by permission.

Reliquiae Baxterianae: or Narrative of His Life and Times, 1:21 by Richard Baxter.

"The Love of God and Affliction," by Simone Weil in *Simone Weil: On Science, Necessity, and the Love of God,* trans. and ed. Richard Rees. Copyright © 1963 Oxford University Press. Reprinted by

CHAPTER 3

CHAPTER 4

A Priest Forever by Carter Heyward. Copyright © 1976 Harper & Row. Reprinted by permission of the author.

Praying Our Goodbyes by Joyce Rupp, OSM. Copyright © 1988 Ave Maria Press. Reprinted by permission.

CHAPTER 5

Moral Fragments and Moral Community: A Proposal for Church in Society by Larry L. Rassmussen. Copyright © 1993 Augsburg Fortress. Reprinted by permission.

"May God's Peace, Mercy and Blessings Be Unto You," by Jean Zaru in *Speaking of Faith: Cross Cultural Perspectives on Women, Religion and Social Change,* ed. Devaki Jain and Diana L. Eck. Copyright © 1986 Kali for Women (India). Reprinted by permission of the publisher and Diana Eck.

With All God's People, 1989. Reprinted by permission of the World Council of Churches (Switzerland).

May 1963 letter by Martin Luther King Jr., cited in Stephen B. Oates, *Let the Trumpet Sound: The Life of Martin Luther King, Jr.* Copyright © 1982 Search Press. Reprinted by permission of Burns and Oates.

"Who Touched Me?" by Consultation of Methodist Women Ministers in *Celebrating Women,* edited by Janet Morely and Hannah Ward. Published by Women in Theology and Movement for the Ordination of Women, 1986, reprinted 1987.

The Wounded Healer by Henri J. M. Nouwen. Copyright © 1972 Henri J. M. Nouwen. Reprinted by permission of Doubleday, a division of Random House, Inc.

He Is Risen by Thomas Merton. Copyright © RCL Enterprises, Inc. Reprinted by permission.

Creative Suffering: The Ripple of Hope by Alan Paton. Copyright © 1970 Pilgrim Press. Reprinted by permission.

Sharing the Darkness by Sheila Cassidy. Copyright © 1991 Orbis Books. Reprinted by permission of Orbis Books and Darton Longman & Todd (UK).

CHAPTER 6

Suffering by Dorothee Sölle. Copyright © 1975 Fortress Press. Reprinted by permission of Augsburg Fortress.

Meditations: Dorothy Day, selected and arranged by Stanley Vishnewskii. Copyright © 1970 The Missionary of Society of St. Paul the Apostle in the State of New York. Reprinted by permission of Tamar Hennessy.

Heart of Joy: The Transforming Power of Self-Giving by Mother Teresa. Copyright © 1987 José Luis González Balado. Reprinted by permission of Servant Publications.

A Rocking Horse Catholic by Caryll Houselander. Copyright © 1955 Sheed & Ward. Reprinted by permission.

Engaging the Powers by Walter Wink. Copyright © 1992 Augsburg Fortress. Reprinted by permission.

"Mary, His Mother, Is Weeping Again in the Plaza del Mayo," from *Ecumenical Decade 1988–1998: Churches in Solidarity with Women.* Reprinted by permission of The World Council of Churches (Switzerland).

The Active Life: A Spirituality of Work, Creativity, and Caring by Parker Palmer. Copyright © 1990 Parker Palmer. Reprinted by permission of HarperCollins Publishers, Inc.

Words Made Flesh: Scripture, Psychology, and Human Communication by Fran Ferder. Copyright © 1986 Ave Maria Press. Reprinted by permission. Used by permission.

What Does the Lord Require of Us? 14ᵗʰ Biennial Convention Worship Resource Book. Copyright © 1989 The National Council of Churches in the Philippines. Reprinted by permission.

"The Feminist Challenge," by Ranjini Rebera in *The Power We Celebrate: Women's Stories of Faith and Power,* eds. Musimbi R. A. Kanyoro and Wendy S. Robins. Copyright © 1992 Lutheran World Federation. Reprinted by permission.

Addiction and Grace by Gerald May. Copyright © 1988 Gerald G. May. Reprinted by permission of HarperCollins Publishers, Inc.

CHAPTER 7

The Mystery and the Passion by David Buttrick. Copyright © 1992 Augsburg Fortress. Reprinted by permission of the author.

Christology at the Crossroads by Jon Sobrino. Copyright © 1978 Orbis Books. Reprinted by permission.

Experiencing God: Theology as Spirituality by Kenneth Leech. Copyright © 1985 Kenneth Leech. Reprinted by permission of HarperCollins Publishers, Inc. and the author.

A Death in Jerusalem by Richard Holloway. Copyright © 1986 Richard Hollway. Reprinted by permission of Morehouse Publishing and HarperCollins (UK).

Lament for a Son by Nicolas Wolterstorff. Copyright © 1987. Reprinted by permission of William B. Eerdmens Publishing, Co. and SPCK (UK).

Philosophical Fragments by Søren Kierkegaard. Copyright © 1936. Reprinted by permission of Princeton University Press.

The Crucified God by Jürgen Moltmann. Copyright © 1974 SCM Press, Ltd. Reprinted by permission of HarperCollins Publishers, Inc., SCM Press (UK), and the author.

"Meditations on the Joy of the Resurrection," by Sergei Nikolaevich Bulgakov in *Ultimate Questions,* ed. Alexander Schmemann. Copyright © 1965 Holt, Rinehart and Winston.

CHAPTER 8

Meister Eckhart, quoted in *Original Blessing* by Matthew Fox. Copyright © 1983 Bear & Co. Reprinted by permission.

"Jesus, You Have Heard Our Tears," from *Bread of Tomorrow* by Janet Morely. Copyright © 1992 Janet Morley. Reprinted by permission.

The Silence of God by Helmut Thielicke. Copyright © 1962 William B. Eerdmans Publishing Co. Reprinted by permission. All rights reserved.

CREDITS

Commentary on Psalm 110 by Martin Luther
from *Luther's Works*, vol. 13. Copyright ©
1956, 1984 Concordia Publishing House.
Reprinted by permission.

Sojourner Truth's Narrative and Book of Life
by Olive Gilbert. Copyright © 1968 Arno
Press. Reprinted by permission of Ayer
Company Publishers.

Campesinos Desplazados, Páginas 12/84
(1987), 6.

CHAPTER 9

Suffering by Dorothee Sölle. Copyright ©
1975 Fortress Press. Reprinted by permission of Augsburg Fortress.

The Form of the Personal by John Macmurray. Copyright © 1961.

The Wounded Healer by Henri J. M. Nouwen.
Copyright © 1972 Henri J. M. Nouwen.
Reprinted by permission of Doubleday, a
division of Random House, Inc.

In the Parish of the Poor: Writings from Haiti
by Jean-Bertrand Aristide. Copyright ©
1990 Orbis Books. Reprinted by permission.

"May God's Peace, Mercy and Blessings Be
Unto You," by Jean Zaru in *Speaking of
Faith: Cross Cultural Perspectives on
Women, Religion and Social Change*, eds.
Devaki Jain and Diana L. Eck. Copyright
© 1986 Kali for Women (India). Reprinted
by permission of the publisher and Diana
Eck.

Showings by Julian of Norwich. Paraphrased
by the editors.

"I Am No Longer Afraid of Death," from
Threatened with Resurrection by Julia
Esquivel. Copyright © 1982, 1994
Brethren Press. Reprinted by permission.

"I Believe," from *Bread of Tomorrow*.
Reprinted by permission of the Method
Church in Britian.

His Life Is Mine by Archimandrite Sophrony.
Copyright © 1977 A. R. Mowbray & Co.
Publishers, Inc. Reprinted by permission of
St. Vladimir's Seminary Press.

"With My Christ," by Nestor of Magydus in
Prayers of the Martyrs, ed. Duane W. H.
Arnold. Copyright © 1991 Duane W. H.
Arnold.

CHAPTER 10

"Persecution of Christians under
Apartheid," by Desmond Tutu in *Martyrdom Today*, eds. Johannes-Baptist Metz
and Edward Schillebeeckx. Copyright ©
1983 Stichting Concilium, T & T Clark
Ltd. and the Seabury Press. Reprinted by
permission.

The Mystery and the Passion by David Buttrick. Copyright © 1992 Augsburg
Fortress. Reprinted by permission of the
author.

"The Martyrs' Living Witness," by Daniel
Berrigan in *Sojourners* magazine, April 1990.
Reprinted by permission of *Sojourners*.

The Church Is All of You by Archbishop
Oscar Romero, comp. and trans. by James
R. Brockman, S.J. Copyright © 1984
Chicago Province of the Society of Jesus.

CHAPTER 13

CHAPTER 14

Index of Sources